Green haven P
# 20.96
P.O. 67128

# DISCARDED

**DATE DUE**

| | |
|---|---|
| | |
| DEC 1 1 2003 | |
| | |
| | |
| | |
| | |
| | |
| | |
| | |
| | |
| | |
| | |
| | |
| | |
| | |

DEMCO, INC. 38-2971

# BUSINESS
# ETHICS

Other Books in the At Issue Series:

# BUSINESS ETHICS

David Bender, *Publisher*
Bruno Leone, *Executive Editor*

Scott Barbour, *Managing Editor*
Brenda Stalcup, *Series Editor*

Tamara L. Roleff, *Book Editor*

An Opposing Viewpoints ® Series

Greenhaven Press, Inc.
San Diego, California

Library of Congress Cataloging-in-Publication Data

Business ethics / Tamara L. Roleff, book editor.
    p.    cm. — (At issue) (An opposing viewpoints series)
    Includes bibliographical references and index.
    ISBN 1-56510-385-8 (lib. : alk. paper) — ISBN 1-56510-384-X
(pbk. : alk. paper)
    1. Business ethics. I. Roleff, Tamara, 1959- . II. Series.
III. Series: Opposing viewpoints series (Unnumbered)
HF5387.B8665   1996
174'.4—dc20                                   95-39052
                                                 CIP

© 1996 by Greenhaven Press, Inc., PO Box 289009,
San Diego, CA 92198-9009

Printed in the U.S.A.

# Table of Contents

# Introduction

In early 1991 Ben & Jerry's Homemade, a Vermont-based ice cream manufacturer, found itself in the unusual position of wanting to pay its suppliers more for their dairy products than the suppliers were charging. Federal price supports for milk had fallen 25 percent, driving prices below farmers' production costs. While most companies would cheer the prospect of lower costs and higher profits, the news was not welcome to Ben Cohen, Ben & Jerry's cofounder. "We would not expect any of our other suppliers to sell to us at prices below their cost of production and we don't expect it of our dairy suppliers, either," Cohen said when he announced the company's decision to pay its dairy suppliers a premium. Ben & Jerry's generosity ended up costing the company $480,000 in 1991—a sum that, according to Cohen, came out of "our profits, where it doesn't belong, and [went] into farmers' pockets, where it does belong."

When Ben Cohen and Jerry Greenfield opened their first Ben & Jerry's ice cream parlor in Burlington, Vermont, in 1978, they did not anticipate that one day their company would be recognized as a leader among socially responsible businesses. While no one definition encompasses all the tenets of corporate social responsibility, most of these companies believe that businesses exist not only to make a profit but to improve the quality of life in local, national, and global communities. These improvements include, but are not limited to, ethical business practices, such as obeying all laws and regulations; environmental conservation and preservation; contributing to the community in the form of donations or volunteer work; providing a safe and fair work environment for workers, including one free from sexual harassment; hiring and promoting women and minorities; and offering employees incentives such as stock ownership so they can share in the wealth they help create.

Cohen believes social responsibility aids both the community and the company. In a 1992 letter to stockholders, Cohen expressed his opinion that social responsibility brings many benefits to companies such as Ben & Jerry's:

> The most amazing thing is that our social values—that part of our company mission statement that calls us to use our power as a business to improve the quality of life in our local, national and international communities—have actually helped us to become a stable, profitable, high-growth company. . . . As we help others, we cannot help helping ourselves.

Cohen claimed that the company's financial success in 1992—a sales increase of 36 percent and a profit increase of 79 percent—was in large part due to the positive public image created by Ben & Jerry's socially responsible business practices.

Another business that has created a public image of social responsibility and community involvement is The Body Shop, a manufacturer and retailer of naturally based cosmetics. Anita Roddick, founder and managing director of The Body Shop, believes that business should be "conducted with love and a powerful force for good." Roddick has built much of The Body Shop's reputation as a socially conscious corporation by championing animal rights, environmentalism, and other social causes. Roddick maintains that one of The Body Shop's primary goals is to give something back to the communities with which it trades and to help the world at large. To this end, the company has established its Trade Not Aid program to buy products from tribal and Third World cultures, and it has built factories and employed workers in impoverished locations around the world. One Trade Not Aid project involves the Kayapo Indians in the Amazon rain forest. In an attempt to provide environmentally sustainable employment for the Kayapo, The Body Shop contracted the tribe to harvest and crush Brazil nuts to obtain an oil that is used in some of the company's products. The Body Shop believes it is helping the global community by working with the Kayapo to develop new products, since the tribe's other economic alternatives—logging, farming, and mining—would threaten the survival of the rain forest.

Other businesses, such as Dayton Hudson Corporation, concentrate on aiding their local communities. One of America's largest retailers, Dayton Hudson donates 5 percent of its pretax profits—rather than the usual 1 to 2 percent most companies give—to arts programs and social causes in the stores' local communities. Kenneth A. Macke, the company's chairman and CEO, maintains that "[Dayton Hudson's] philosophy has always been that we exist to serve society—not just to make money. I prefer to focus on what Dayton Hudson can do to change things and set an example. The Dayton family built this company on a broad definition of success: We succeed when we are good stewards for all stakeholders."

The business policies of Ben & Jerry's, The Body Shop, and Dayton Hudson—and the principles behind them—run counter to the beliefs of most capitalists, economists, and business owners. Their philosophy is best expressed by former president Calvin Coolidge's famous maxim: "The business of business is business." Critics of corporate social responsibility believe that a business's sole responsibility is to make money for its owners, not to solve the world's problems. To willingly pay a vendor more than the asking price, to build a plant in a city merely because it has a high unemployment rate, or to support the local symphony all go against the traditional business policy of maximizing profits and providing a higher rate of return for the companies' owners and investors.

In a June 1991 article in *Fortune* magazine, Daniel Seligman argued that Ben & Jerry's philanthropic gesture toward Vermont farmers ended up costing the company's customers. Although Ben & Jerry's absorbed the $480,000 loss incurred by this particular decision, Seligman believes that, on the whole, Ben & Jerry's corporate social responsibility causes their customers to pay more for their ice cream. According to Seligman, businesses can help their communities most by providing goods and services at the lowest possible price: "A mere profit maximizer would doubtless do less for Indian berry pickers [who pick blueberries for Wild Maine Blueberry ice cream]. But more for [Ben & Jerry's] customers." His comment echoed a statement that appeared in *Fortune* almost 20 years earlier. In a June 1973 *Fortune* article, the editors maintained, "A businessman can hardly find a better measure of his contribution to social welfare than his own profits."

The views of *Fortune*'s editors are consistent with those of economist and Nobel laureate Milton Friedman, who asserts that the primary responsibility of business managers is to make as much money for the owners as is legally possible. If a CEO donates part of the firm's profits to an outside cause—worthy or not—the CEO is taking a percentage of the profits that would otherwise go to the stockholders, Friedman contends. By making decisions for the stockholders on how to spend their money and by spending it differently than the stockholders might have, Friedman maintains, the CEO is in fact taking over a government function: taxation. The stockholders' diminished returns are a result of this taxation, he claims. Furthermore, Friedman argues, this taxation is without representation, since the stockholders have not authorized the company to give away their profits.

Other critics contend that many companies fail to live up to their own standards of social responsibility. For example in September 1994 Jon Entine wrote in *Business Ethics* that rather than using primarily natural and renewable ingredients, "The Body Shop uses many outdated, off-the-shelf product formulas filled with nonrenewable petrochemicals." According to Entine, the company has also "increased its use of ingredients that at some point have been tested on animals despite high-profile opposition to animal testing." Entine contends that although The Body Shop heavily promotes its Trade Not Aid program, the natural ingredients obtained from rain forest Indians and other tribal people actually make up a very small percentage of the overall ingredients in its products. Furthermore, David Moberg maintains in the September 19, 1994, issue of *In These Times*, that The Body Shop actually exploits workers in its Trade Not Aid program. He claims that the income the Kayapo tribe receives from The Body Shop for harvesting Brazil nuts is "meager" and "has never provided a real alternative to the revenue the Kayapo earn from signing contracts with logging and mining corporations." The Body Shop is just one example, critics charge, of multinational companies that misrepresent the extent of their social responsibility in order to promote their own image—a practice these critics consider unethical.

As consumers both at home and abroad demand to know the story behind the product and the producer, business ethics and social responsibility will become more of an issue. Business ethicists will demand that companies contribute to society, while economists and capitalists will insist that a firm's only debt is to its owners. In *At Issue: Business Ethics*, authors debate whether businesses have an incentive and a duty to be socially responsible.

# 1

# Milton Friedman's Case Against Corporate Social Responsibility

## Milton Friedman

*Milton Friedman, a Nobel laureate in economics, wrote what many consider to be the classic argument against corporate social responsibility in 1970. More than twenty-five years later, business writers are still debating the merits and demerits of this concept. Friedman is a senior research fellow at the Hoover Institution, a research organization devoted to domestic and international affairs, at Stanford University in Palo Alto, California. He is the author of* Capitalism and Freedom *and* Free to Choose *and is a contributing editor for* Newsweek.

The primary responsibility of a corporate executive is to serve the owners of the business. As the owners' agent, it is his responsibility to conduct business in accordance with their desires, mainly the desire to make as much money as possible. Corporate social responsibility is not in the interest of the company's owners because it costs the owners money and reduces their profits. Some companies may choose to provide amenities to a community because it is in their interest to do so, but it is hypocritical for executives to claim these actions are examples of social responsibility.

When I hear businessmen speak eloquently about the "social responsibilities of business in a free-enterprise system," I am reminded of the wonderful line about the Frenchman who discovered at the age of 70 that he had been speaking prose all his life. The businessmen believe that they are defending free enterprise when they declaim that business is not concerned "merely" with profit but also with promoting desirable "social" ends; that business has a "social conscience" and takes seriously its responsibilities for providing employment, eliminating discrimination, avoiding pollution and whatever else may be the catchwords of the contemporary crop of reformers. In fact they are—or would be if they or anyone else took them seriously—preaching pure and unadulterated social-

Milton Friedman, "The Social Responsibility of Business Is to Increase Its Profits," *New York Times Sunday Magazine*, September 13, 1970. Copyright ©1970 by The New York Times Company. Reprinted by permission.

ism. Businessmen who talk this way are unwitting puppets of the intellectual forces that have been undermining the basis of a free society these past decades.

The discussions of the "social responsibilities of business" are notable for their analytical looseness and lack of rigor. What does it mean to say that "business" has responsibilities? Only people can have responsibilities. A corporation is an artificial person and in this sense may have artificial responsibilities, but "business" as a whole cannot be said to have responsibilities, even in this vague sense. The first step toward clarity in examining the doctrine of the social responsibility of business is to ask precisely what it implies for whom.

Presumably, the individuals who are to be responsible are businessmen, which means individual proprietors or corporate executives. Most of the discussion of social responsibility is directed at corporations, so in what follows I shall mostly neglect the individual proprietor and speak of corporate executives.

## The business owners' agent

In a free-enterprise, private-property system, a corporate executive is an employee of the owners of the business. He has direct responsibility to his employers. That responsibility is to conduct the business in accordance with their desires, which generally will be to make as much money as possible while conforming to the basic rules of the society, both those embodied in law and those embodied in ethical custom. Of course, in some cases his employers may have a different objective. A group of persons might establish a corporation for an eleemosynary [charitable] purpose—for example, a hospital or a school. The manager of such a corporation will not have money profit as his objective but the rendering of certain services.

In either case, the key point is that, in his capacity as a corporate executive, the manager is the agent of the individuals who own the corporation or establish the eleemosynary institution, and his primary responsibility is to them.

> *The manager is the agent of the individuals who own the corporation . . . and his primary responsibility is to them.*

Needless to say, this does not mean that it is easy to judge how well he is performing his task. But at least the criterion of performance is straightforward, and the persons among whom a voluntary contractual arrangement exists are clearly defined.

Of course, the corporate executive is also a person in his own right. As a person, he may have many other responsibilities that he recognizes or assumes voluntarily—to his family, his conscience, his feelings of charity, his church, his clubs, his city, his country. He may feel impelled by these responsibilities to devote part of his income to causes he regards as worthy, to refuse to work for particular corporations, even to leave his job, for example, to join his country's armed forces. If we wish, we may refer to some of these responsibilities as "social responsibilities." But in these respects he is acting as a principal, not an agent; he is spending his own money or time or energy, not the money of his employers or the time or energy he has contracted to devote to their purposes. If these are "social responsibilities," they are the social responsibilities of individuals, not of business.

---

*The conflict of interest is naked and clear when union officials are asked to subordinate the interest of their members to some more general social purpose.*

---

What does it mean to say that the corporate executive has a "social responsibility" in his capacity as businessman? If this statement is not pure rhetoric, it must mean that he is to act in some way that is not in the interest of his employers. For example, that he is to refrain from increasing the price of the product in order to contribute to the social objective of preventing inflation, even though a price increase would be in the best interests of the corporation. Or that he is to make expenditures on reducing pollution beyond the amount that is in the best interests of the corporation or that is required by law in order to contribute to the social objective of improving the environment. Or that, at the expense of corporate profits, he is to hire "hard-core" unemployed instead of better-qualified available workmen to contribute to the social objective of reducing poverty.

In each of these cases, the corporate executive would be spending someone else's money for a general social interest. Insofar as his actions in accord with his "social responsibility" reduce returns to stockholders, he is spending their money. Insofar as his actions raise the price to customers, he is spending the customers' money. Insofar as his actions lower the wages of some employees, he is spending their money.

The stockholders or the customers or the employees could separately spend their own money on the particular action if they wished to do so. The executive is exercising a distinct "social responsibility," rather than serving as an agent of the stockholders or the customers or the employees, only if he spends the money in a different way than they would have spent it.

But if he does this, he is in effect imposing taxes, on the one hand, and deciding how the tax proceeds shall be spent, on the other.

## Taxation without representation

This process raises political questions on two levels: principle and consequences. On the level of political principle, the imposition of taxes and the expenditure of tax proceeds are governmental functions. We have established elaborate constitutional, parliamentary and judicial provisions to control these functions, to assure that taxes are imposed so far as possible in accordance with the preferences and desires of the public—after all, "taxation without representation" was one of the battle cries of the American Revolution. We have a system of checks and balances to separate the legislative function of imposing taxes and enacting expenditures from the executive function of collecting taxes and administering expenditure programs and from the judicial function of mediating disputes and interpreting the law.

Here the businessman—self-selected or appointed directly or indirectly by stockholders—is to be simultaneously legislator, executive and jurist. He is to decide whom to tax by how much and for what purpose, and he is to spend the proceeds—all this guided only by general exhortations from on high to restrain inflation, improve the environment, fight poverty and so on and on.

---

*The use of the cloak of social responsibility . . . does clearly harm the foundations of a free society.*

---

The whole justification for permitting the corporate executive to be selected by the stockholders is that the executive is an agent serving the interests of his principal. This justification disappears when the corporate executive imposes taxes and spends the proceeds for "social" purposes. He becomes in effect a public employee, a civil servant, even though he remains in name an employee of a private enterprise. On grounds of political principle, it is intolerable that such civil servants—insofar as their actions in the name of social responsibility are real and not just window-dressing—should be selected as they are now. If they are to be civil servants, then they must be selected through a political process. If they are to impose taxes and make expenditures to foster "social" objectives, then political machinery must be set up to guide the assessment of taxes and to determine through a political process the objectives to be served.

This is the basic reason why the doctrine of "social responsibility" involves the acceptance of the socialist view that political mechanisms, not market mechanisms, are the appropriate way to determine the allocation of scarce resources to alternative uses.

On the grounds of consequences, can the corporate executive in fact discharge his alleged "social responsibilities"? On the one hand, suppose he could get away with spending the stockholders' or customers' or employees' money. How is he to know how to spend it? He is told that he must contribute to fighting inflation. How is he to know what action of his will contribute to that end? He is presumably an expert in running his company—in producing a product or selling it or financing it. But nothing about his selection makes him an expert on inflation. Will his holding down the price of his product reduce inflationary pressure? Or, by leaving more spending power in the hands of his customers, simply divert it elsewhere? Or, by forcing him to produce less because of the lower price, will it simply contribute to shortages? Even if he could answer these questions, how much cost is he justified in imposing on his stockholders, customers and employees for this social purpose? What is his appropriate share and what is the appropriate share of others?

And, whether he wants to or not, can he get away with spending his stockholders', customers' or employees' money? Will not the stockholders fire him? (Either the present ones or those who take over when his actions in the name of social responsibility have reduced the corporation's profits and the price of its stock.) His customers and his employees can desert him for other producers and employers less scrupulous in exercising their social responsibilities.

This facet of "social responsibility" doctrine is brought into sharp relief when the doctrine is used to justify wage restraint by trade unions. The conflict of interest is naked and clear when union officials are asked to subordinate the interest of their members to some more general social purpose. If the union officials try to enforce wage restraint, the consequence is likely to be wildcat strikes, rank-and-file revolts and the emergence of strong competitors for their jobs. We thus have the ironic phenomenon that union leaders—at least in the U.S.—have objected to government interference with the market far more consistently and courageously than have business leaders.

The difficulty of exercising "social responsibility" illustrates, of course, the great virtue of private competitive enterprise—it forces people to be responsible for their own actions and makes it difficult for them to "exploit" other people for either selfish or unselfish purposes. They can do good—but only at their own expense.

Many a reader who has followed the argument this far may be tempted to remonstrate that it is all well and good to speak of government's having the responsibility to impose taxes and determine expenditures for such "social" purposes as controlling pollution or training the hard-core unemployed, but that the problems are too urgent to wait on the slow course of political processes, that the exercise of social responsibility by businessmen is a quicker and surer way to solve pressing current problems.

## An undemocratic procedure

Aside from the question of fact—I share Adam Smith's skepticism about the benefits that can be expected from "those who affected to trade for the public good"—this argument must be rejected on grounds of principle. What it amounts to is an assertion that those who favor the taxes and expenditures in question have failed to persuade a majority of their fellow citizens to be of like mind and that they are seeking to attain by undemocratic procedures what they cannot attain by democratic procedures. In a free society, it is hard for "good" people to do "good," but that is a small price to pay for making it hard for "evil" people to do "evil," especially since one man's good is another's evil.

I have, for simplicity, concentrated on the special case of the corporate executive, except only for the brief digression on trade unions. But precisely the same argument applies to the newer phenomenon of calling upon stockholders to require corporations to exercise social responsibility. In most of these cases, what is in effect involved is some stockholders trying to get other stockholders (or customers or employees) to contribute against their will to "social" causes favored by the activists. Insofar as they succeed, they are again imposing taxes and spending the proceeds.

The situation of the individual proprietor is somewhat different. If he acts to reduce the returns of his enterprise in order to exercise his "social responsibility," he is spending his own money, not someone else's. If he wishes to spend his money on such purposes, that is his right, and I cannot see that there is any objection to his doing so. In the process, he, too, may impose costs on employees and customers. However, because he is far less likely than a large corporation or union to have monopolistic power, any such side effects will tend to be minor.

Of course, in practice the doctrine of social responsibility is frequently a cloak for actions that are justified on other grounds rather than a reason for those actions.

---

*There is one and only one social responsibility of business—to use its resources and engage in activities designed to increase its profits.*

---

To illustrate, it may well be in the long-run interest of a corporation that is a major employer in a small community to devote resources to providing amenities to that community or to improving its government. That may make it easier to attract desirable employees, it may reduce the wage bill or lessen losses from pilferage and sabotage or have other worthwhile effects. Or it may be that, given the laws about the deductibility of corporate charitable contributions, the stockholders can contribute more to charities they favor by having the corporation make the gift than by doing it themselves, since they can in that way contribute an amount that would otherwise have been paid as corporate taxes.

In each of these—and many similar—cases, there is a strong temptation to rationalize these actions as an exercise of "social responsibility." In the present climate of opinion, with its widespread aversion to "capitalism," "profits," the "soulless corporation" and so on, this is one way for a corporation to generate goodwill as a by-product of expenditures that are entirely justified in its own self-interest.

It would be inconsistent of me to call on corporate executives to refrain from this hypocritical window-dressing because it harms the foundations of a free society. That would be to call on them to exercise a "social responsibility"! If our institutions, and the attitudes of the public, make it in their self-interest to cloak their actions in this way, I cannot summon much indignation to denounce them. At the same time, I can express admiration for those individual proprietors or owners of closely held corporations or stockholders of more broadly held corporations who disdain such tactics as approaching fraud.

Whether blameworthy or not, the use of the cloak of social responsibility, and the nonsense spoken in its name by influential and prestigious businessmen, does clearly harm the foundations of a free society. I have been impressed time and again by the schizophrenic character of many businessmen. They are capable of being extremely far-sighted and clearheaded in matters that are internal to their businesses. They are incredibly short-sighted and muddle-headed in matters that are outside their businesses but affect the possible survival of business in general. This short-sightedness is strikingly exemplified in the calls from many businessmen for wage and price guidelines or controls or incomes policies. There is nothing that could do more in a brief period to destroy a market system and replace it by a centrally controlled system than effective governmental control of prices and wages.

The short-sightedness is also exemplified in speeches by businessmen on social responsibility. This may gain them kudos in the short run. But it helps to strengthen the already too prevalent view that the pursuit of profits is wicked and immoral and must be curbed and controlled by external forces. Once this view is adopted, the external forces that curb the market will not be the social consciences, however highly developed, of the pontificating executives; it will be the iron fist of government bureaucrats. Here, as with price and wage controls, businessmen seem to me to reveal a suicidal impulse.

The political principle that underlies the market mechanism is unanimity. In an ideal free market resting on private property, no individual can coerce any other, all cooperation is voluntary, all parties to such cooperation benefit or they need not participate. There are no "social" values, no "social" responsibilities in any sense other than the shared values and responsibilities of individuals. Society is a collection of individuals and of the various groups they voluntarily form.

The political principle that underlies the political mechanism is conformity. The individual must serve a more general social interest—whether that be determined by a church or a dictator or a majority. The individual may have a vote and a say in what is to be done, but if he is overruled, he must conform. It is appropriate for some to require others to contribute to a general social purpose whether they wish to or not.

Unfortunately, unanimity is not always feasible. There are some respects in which conformity appears unavoidable, so I do not see how one can avoid the use of the political mechanism altogether.

But the doctrine of "social responsibility" taken seriously would extend the scope of the political mechanism to every human activity. It does not differ in philosophy from the most explicitly collectivist doctrine. It differs only by professing to believe that collectivist ends can be attained without collectivist means. That is why, in my book *Capitalism and Freedom*, I have called it a "fundamentally subversive doctrine" in a free society, and have said that in such a society, "there is one and only one social responsibility of business—to use its resources and engage in activities designed to increase its profits so long as it stays within the rules of the game, which is to say, engages in open and free competition without deception or fraud."

# Corporate Social Responsibility Benefits Business

## Alan Reder

*Alan Reder is the coauthor of* Investing from the Heart: The Guide to Socially Responsible Investments and Money Management *and the author of* In Pursuit of Principle and Profit: Business Success Through Social Responsibility, *from which this viewpoint is excerpted.*

Adherents to the philosophy of corporate social responsibility believe that business should be conducted in a way that has a positive impact on society, the economy, and the environment. More and more businesses are discovering that conserving resources, protecting the environment, treating their employees fairly, becoming involved in their community's activities, and other socially responsible policies make good business sense. They find that corporate social responsibility may improve their bottom line as well as result in increased employee allegiance, productivity, and work quality; management insight and creativity; and customer loyalty.

In an old Jack Benny routine, a mugger stops the frugal comic and demands, "Your money or your life!" For several long moments, Benny says nothing. The mugger snaps, "Well?" Benny answers, "Don't rush me, I'm thinking, I'm thinking!"

We often accuse business leaders of having a similarly misplaced sense of priorities, but they can't be entirely blamed when money—specifically, profit—is the lifeblood of their game. A company won't long survive if it doesn't ultimately take in at least somewhat more than it pays out.

Of course, a business's profitability depends upon it attaining any number of subgoals. Conventional management wisdom tells us that a company's ultimate success results from such attributes as
- The creation of products and services that are wanted and needed in the marketplace

Reprinted by permission of The Putnam Publishing Group/Jeremy P. Tarcher, Inc., from *In Pursuit of Principle and Profit* by Alan Reder. Copyright ©1994 by Alan Reder.

- Employees who are skilled and knowledgeable, particularly with the demands of today's global, high-technology economy; who are loyal, because high work-force turnover is both disruptive and exceptionally costly; and who, at minimum, do not undermine the company's goals with below-par workmanship and customer service
- A management team that understands how to inspire both that work force to perform competently and customers to purchase the company's output

That's just for starters. Executives know that companies that rise above the competition often distinguish themselves in other ways.

- Their employees are unusually productive and efficient, caring for the company as if it were their own; or
- Employees at all levels contribute creatively to the business, offering practical, innovative, money-making or money-saving ideas; or
- Management is uncommonly sensitive and responsive to changes in today's almost continually transforming marketplace; or
- Customers actually delight in buying the company's products and services and love to talk them up to other potential customers

Notice that social responsibility hasn't been mentioned yet. Placing it this high on a goals list probably wouldn't occur to the average manager, even one motivated to "do the right thing" whenever possible. However, as you will see, social responsibility helps ensure that virtually every quality of a successful company will emerge over time, and thus greatly increases a company's chances of long-term success.

Of course, it's much easier to pontificate about social responsibility in business than to get specific about what it means. Speaking at a 1993 conference I attended in Atlanta, Kirk Hanson, Stanford University Graduate School of Business lecturer and first president of The Business Enterprise Trust, an organization that honors exemplary business behavior, noted: "I don't think we [in the socially responsible business movement] have been able yet to articulate the overall vision of what business responsibility is. When people go to look for that overall vision, they sometimes think it's the 1960s agenda. Maybe it's the political agenda of a particular administration. Sometimes, they think it's whatever's on Ralph's [Nader, another conference presenter] mind that day and what his particular programmatic concerns are."

Kirk's right. My friends and acquaintances in the socially responsible business community include some individuals who are as distrustful of government regulation and big government in general as any Fortune 500 Republican, although they would likely break with their conservative counterparts on most issues involving business's obligations to society. I belong to the Social Venture Network (SVN), a leading national organization of socially conscious business leaders (the group, in fact, that Hanson was addressing), but I don't know of any poll that's ever been taken of members' social attitudes. Besides, many of these folks are so iconoclastic and creative in their thinking that I don't think a poll could capture them.

Therefore, much of what I will label "socially responsible" below has not been submitted to a vote by any policy committee. But this label does reflect to a large extent the public behavior and explicit mission statements of many of these companies. Accounting for inevitable differences between organizations, it also reflects criteria that the socially responsible investment community, in which I traffic as well, uses to screen stocks and other investments for their clientele. Assume that unless otherwise credited, further articulation of these categories is my own.

---

*Social responsibility helps ensure that virtually every quality of a successful company will emerge over time, and thus greatly increases a company's chances of long-term success.*

---

An all-encompassing notion, social responsibility refers to both the way a company conducts its internal operations, including the way it treats its work force, and its impact on the world around it. Most socially responsible business and investment leaders endeavor to further the following agenda of ethical policies and practices:
- Reducing to the greatest degree possible the damage a company causes the environment
- Contributing in every conceivable way to environmental preservation, through resource conservation and energy efficiency, through environmentally conscious purchases and product design, through publicly auditing its environmental performance, and so on
- Not doing business in repressive regimes such as South Africa was prior to the ending of apartheid and such as Burma is today
- For companies doing defense contracting, not lobbying for the sale of weaponry to unstable regimes, otherwise resisting the classic military-industrial complex temptations, and converting to peacetime industries to the greatest degree possible in a post–Cold War world
- Aggressively hiring and promoting women and minorities, including to the company's upper management positions and board of directors
- Providing employees with a safe, clean, healthy work environment
- Helping employees care for their children and dependent elderly family members through such arrangements as dependent care assistance and flexible time
- Protecting employees from sexual harassment
- Fairly compensating employees for their labors and not undermining employees' right to organize
- Providing permanent, domestic jobs to the greatest degree possible
- Not exploiting campaign finance and lobbying laws for narrow corporate ends
- Obeying all laws and regulations affecting the company's industry
- Conducting international business in a nonexploitive manner and a manner consistent with the company's stateside policies and practices
- Humanely treating animals, including not testing products on them when appropriate alternatives exist
- Allowing employees to share the wealth they help generate through stock ownership, incentive pay, or other means

- Encouraging employees at all levels to contribute ideas and participate in critical company decision-making
- Giving something back, in the form of charity or voluntary community involvement, to the community and society in which the company does business
- Purchasing in the most socially conscientious manner possible, including contracting with minority- and women-owned companies and applying environmental standards to vendor relationships
- Designing high-quality, durable products that are safe for the consumer and make a beneficial impact on society
- Marketing products or services only in socially appropriate manners (i.e., not exploiting ethnic and gender stereotypes, not exploiting vulnerable markets such as children or Third World populations, and so on)

This still partial list ignores many specific points. Nevertheless, it does demonstrate the range of activities encompassed by the term "social responsibility," a wide range indeed because social responsibility implies conscientious attention to every conceivable social impact of a company's activities. Most items on the list run absolutely counter to conservative economist Milton Friedman's oft-quoted line that "the business of business is business." They run counter as well to the protests of many corporate leaders that environmental restrictions, family-leave legislation, safety regulations, giving employees stock in the company and a voice in decisions, and such impair a company's ability to compete.

---

*Good company behavior makes for good business.*

---

However, the chorus of protesters has grown less robust as its numbers shrink. Many managers and company owners who first implemented socially responsible policies and practices simply as a matter of principle have reaped rewards in the form of improved employee allegiance, productivity, and work quality; management insight and creativity; and customer loyalty. As Arnold Hiatt, former chairman of Stride Rite Corporation and leading spokesman for the "enlightened self-interest" approach to social responsibility, told *Newsweek*:

> We look at public service as an investment. We believe the well-being of a company cannot be separated from the well-being of the community. If we're not providing the community with access to day care and eldercare, if we're not providing proper funding for education, then we're not investing properly in our business. . . . [As for the costs], take our family-leave policy. It costs us next to nothing. And yet the statement it makes to employees is powerful. It says to them that we care. And when employees know you care about them, they tend to be more productive. It's the same with our day care. To me, its a no-brainer.

The burgeoning socially responsible investment field has also maintained that good company behavior makes for good business. The best evidence to support their claim has been the steady performance of socially responsible mutual funds and stock portfolios. Many of the socially responsible mutual funds have outperformed the average funds in their investment category over the long term. In single years, some have led the nation. Despite the inevitable runts, the field overall demonstrates that social investors need not concede any profits to invest in socially responsible companies. One implication is that picking stocks by applying both ethical and financial criteria identifies a high percentage of well-run companies.

The above are just a few items in a growing list of evidence suggesting that many companies that are doing well today are doing so in large part because of their socially responsible policies and practices. Their success also implies that those companies that have not implemented socially responsible practices might well improve their performance by taking that step.

## An idea whose time is overdue

However economists and executives regard the socially responsible business approach, time is running out on unprincipled business behavior because of the pace of social change and environmental decay. Whether or not global warming turns out to be scientific fact, the climate, as far as business is concerned, has changed forever. Consider that

- Women and minorities now constitute most entrants into the labor force.
- Minorities are becoming such a huge proportion of the general population that the very term "minority" may be meaningless by the middle of next century.
- Human activity has already exceeded the planet's carrying capacity, according to several leading environmental experts.
- The extinction of many valuable resources, American old-growth timber and Third World rainforest hardwoods among them, is now within sight, and scarcity of potable water has already begun to occur in several nations including the U.S.
- Increasingly significant numbers of consumers are applying social criteria to their purchasing decisions.
- The federal government, saddled with $4 trillion in debt, and the strapped governments of many states find themselves incapable of addressing major social problems, at least in ways requiring large infusions of dollars. This leaves corporate America with the uncomfortable challenge of maintaining earnings in a decaying social milieu unless it finds a way to help reverse the decline.
- Many of today's dominant industries—forestry, chemical-based agriculture, petroleum, beef cattle–raising, passenger vehicle manufacture, to name just a few—are based on socially untenable premises and processes. In other words, their supposed economic viability has been figured without taking into consideration environmental and other societal costs, costs that society will soon determine it can no longer afford. In fact, the besieged forestry industry is already experiencing the effects of such resistance. Speeding the approach of their obsolescence is the fact that each of the industries mentioned could be replaced or retired today with environmentally appropriate alternatives. In fact, the forestry industry has quietly pursued a transition to nontimber paper fibers

and alternative wood products such as manufactured lumber even as it loudly campaigns to chain-saw the rest of America's trees.

## Making a difference

The Body Shop and Ben & Jerry's Homemade stories have been related almost as often as tales of young Abe Lincoln reading by candlelight. These outstanding business citizens remain, despite the occasional contrary impression conveyed by cynical reporters, preeminent examples of "values-driven businesses," or in less formal terms, what Ben & Jerry's calls "caring capitalists." Virtual legends on the basis of incendiary growth alone, these companies not only make few social compromises, relative to mainstream firms anyway, but devote considerable energy and resources to aggressive social initiatives.

Stonyfield Farm Yogurt's story, although not nearly as widely known, is hardly less inspiring. Co-founders Samuel Kaymen and Gary Hirshberg started the New Hampshire–based business in 1983 not to become international yogurt moguls but to fund educational efforts in sustainable agriculture and other appropriate rural technologies. Hanging on with their fingernails to the romance of a farm-based enterprise, Kaymen, his wife, Louise, and Hirshberg milked the cows at the Kaymens' hilltop farm in Wilton, in addition to making and delivering the yogurt, financing the business, and running a nonprofit farm school.

However, the yogurt was so good that demand began to crowd out the romance. In 1984, they let the herd go and started buying milk from local farmers. By 1988, they had outgrown the picturesque farm entirely, and moved the operation to a custom-designed yogurt works in nearby Londonderry.

If exceptional quality had gotten them this far, a broader approach to social responsibility was about to carry them to the top strata of their industry. In 1989, Stonyfield Farm began to invest more heavily "in our people, in our facilities, in basically making the place happier," CEO Hirshberg told me when we spoke in early 1994. "We also poured more money into our cause-related efforts on behalf of family farms and sustainable agriculture. And that's when we turned the corner." Stonyfield started growing at a clip of 50 percent per year, a pace it had maintained for five years running as of this writing in January 1994.

"We're far and away the fastest growing yogurt company in the country if not the world," Gary said. "That fifty percent is top-line growth, but we're also showing fantastic bottom-line results. I think that our success is a result of a whole bunch of things that we're doing and you couldn't pull away any of them and achieve the same levels."

Since every Stonyfield socially responsible policy or practice seems to have played its part in the company's explosive growth, let's dissect the combination. Social responsibility, of course, starts at home with how you treat your employees. In at least one area—career advancement—few treat them better than Stonyfield. In 1993, *Inc.* magazine named Stonyfield as one of the best small companies to work for in America for its commitment to internally post all new job opportunities and hire from within whenever possible. As of this writing, nineteen of twenty-two Stonyfield managers were promoted from within the organization, including production manager Ed Souza, a former limousine driver who started as a yogurt checker five years before.

You don't have to be a supervisor at Stonyfield to share in the goodies. Thanks to the leadership's dedication to open communication, employees at all levels have the opportunity to contribute ideas, on everything from planning and management to plant design, and to hear in detail what's going on with the company financially. The latter particularly intrigues them because the company pays incentives, in the form of cash bonuses and stock options, ranging from between 18 and 23 percent of pretax profits. Employees can also determine their own benefit package, through participation in a benefits committee that surveys the staff on their preferences.

Terrific employee relations don't by themselves define a socially responsible company, and they don't define Stonyfield. Conceivably, a company might lavish stock, high pay, and lovely work conditions on its work force only to make employees feel ashamed of their jobs because of a venally conceived product or environmental practice. Instead, this company's slogan to its customers, "We make you feel good inside," could apply to the way employees feel about their employer, as well as the product their labor produces. Stonyfield Farm's yogurt is not an entirely organic product because making it so would price it far beyond what even health purists have shown they're willing to pay. But it is as wholesome and chemical-free as it can be in current market conditions, which is why you'll find it in so many health food store refrigerators.

---

*Our success is a result of a whole bunch of things that we're doing and you couldn't pull away any of them and achieve the same levels.*

---

One of America's most charitably minded outfits, Stonyfield donated over 7 percent of profits to civic, charitable, and arts organizations in fiscal year 1993. For fiscal year 1994, the company has committed over 5 percent of revenues to advance the cause of sustainable agriculture, and 14 percent of net profits to environmental causes overall, including the premium they pay to buy milk from local farmers using sustainable methods.

Stonyfield's public citizenship doesn't end with the relatively simple act of writing checks. Hirshberg, a trustee of the Audubon Society of New Hampshire, helped found Audubon Associates, an organization of business leaders that meets on environmental issues. The company also works with other corporate sponsors to support New Hampshire arts and humanities and is an active member of three organizations—the Social Venture Network, Businesses for Social Responsibility, and New England Businesses for Social Responsibility—dedicated to advancing socially responsible business practices here and around the world.

Environmentally, Stonyfield has completed an energy audit of its production facility for the purpose of upgrading it to a demonstration-quality energy efficient plant; has hired an environmental auditor to help the company reduce all of its other environmental impacts; and is organizing other food manufacturers using similar plastic packaging to create a recycling infrastructure for its yogurt containers.

On behalf of the health of its customers and survival of its small dairy suppliers, Stonyfield has also campaigned against federal approval of bovine growth hormone (BGH). The hormone, which requires an increased use of antibiotics for dairy herds, may lead to contamination of the milk supply. It could also drive numerous family farms out of business by creating a milk surplus, thus further concentrating America's food supply in the hands of large, environmentally destructive agribusiness. Among myriad other environmental initiatives, Stonyfield has also dedicated a yogurt flavor, Guava Papaya, to the preservation of Amazon rainforest and the indigenous cultures living there.

---

*The economic benefits of the company's social stance help further its mission.*

---

As Hirshberg presented the numbers to me, the company dedicates some 30 percent of profits to its social mission and obviously considerable human energy besides. That's not the usual formula for success, especially for a still relatively small business. But it works for Stonyfield. As Gary put it, "Our happy employees make better yogurt and make customers feel better. So there's no question to me or to anybody here—you could ask anyone in the company—that morale here is very high and really contributes to our success." One unmistakable sign of that high morale: almost nonexistent turnover, about one employee per year, Gary estimates, although he acknowledges that pressure has increased with the pace of growth.

Skeptics will undoubtedly point to the marketing advantages of Stonyfield's highly visible community initiatives. Indeed, like The Body Shop, Stonyfield does no advertising, while benefiting from frequent free, positive press coverage. But Hirshberg stresses that the economic benefits of the company's social stance help further its mission: "I think a litmus test of all socially responsible practices is that they be win-win. They've got to be more profitable. Otherwise, they're not going to pass the test of time."

Stonyfield's example would boast little more than curiosity value if it were unique. But it is not. A growing number of successful American businesses define themselves as idealistically as does Stonyfield and then proceed to walk their talk. Many, such as Patagonia, Esprit, Aveda, South Shore Bank, and Tom's of Maine, have begun to take their places beside Ben & Jerry's and The Body Shop in the iconography of conscientious companies.

And just beneath this tier of high-ideals businesses are a number of successful major American corporations who, while defining their social goals more modestly, still seek to balance their profit-making charge with their social roles as influential organizational citizens. Pitney Bowes, for one, seems to have found no conflict between large market shares and profits, on the one hand, and ethical management, on the other. The company not only hires a high percentage of women and minorities but promotes them as well. Its 23,669 U.S. employees include 8,722 women and 6,425 minority workers. Among the 2,746 regarded as upper management, there are 714 women and 354 minority employees. This equal opportunity attitude extends into Pitney Bowes' purchasing activities: It purchased 13.8 million in products and services from minority-owned firms in 1993.

Among work and family policies instituted before the 1993 family leave legislation, the company offers primary caregivers 90 days of unpaid leave beyond typical leave, runs a childcare resources and referral program, and allows flexible time to be negotiated between employees and supervisors. On the environmental front, three full-time staff—the director of Corporate Safety and Environmental Affairs, the manager of Corporate Environmental Engineering, and the corporate hygienist—monitor the company's environmental performance, including its waste minimization program. The company has put itself on the line with a publicly announced goal of zero discharge of hazardous pollutants by 1996.

Today, corporate campaign contributions have virtually crowded the interests of individual citizen voters, not to mention the general public interest, off the political stage. Pitney Bowes can't by itself change the equation but, on principle, its executives refuse to play. The company gives no money to PACs and its corporate credo bans the backing of political candidates.

Pitney Bowes is no more alone in its league than Stonyfield is on its turf. In addition to several corporate citizens with strong all-around ethical records such as Levi Strauss, Southwest Airlines, Federal Express, Donnelly Corporation, and Fel-Pro, several major corporations have demonstrated, in particular aspects of their operations, the economic attributes of socially responsible practices even if the company as a whole can't be held up as exemplary. For example, Reebok, with its human rights code for overseas business relationships, argues for a new social compact in the global economy.

## Social responsibility: a process, not a position

Earlier, I rendered a preliminary laundry list of socially responsible business behaviors. But Gary Hirshberg, for one, is under no illusion that social responsibility describes any special moral high ground: "We've realized that there isn't any black and white out there when it comes to being socially responsible or environmentally responsible. There's just a whole lot of gray. My idealism is still very much alive but the ultimate irony of a Stonyfield is that maybe less resources would be consumed if we didn't exist. We confront this dilemma daily."

In fact, the enormity of the environmental challenge to even conscientious companies keeps most of the socially responsible business leaders I know fairly humble. It might be philosophically tidy to define socially responsible business behavior as behavior that does not harm society, but that doesn't hold up in practical terms. Nearly all manufacturing, for example, involves some piggish level of energy use and probably other forms of waste and pollution as well. Even environmental organizations have to swallow hard over the trees they devour when they do mass mailings about, say, forest preservation. *Sierra* magazine analyzed its own product in late 1993 and discovered to its horror that, among other disturbing impacts, publishing the magazine resulted in the leveling of old-growth forest.

It's also impossible to describe behavior that doesn't harm society without first limiting how you define society. Business affects many constituencies: employees, customers, stockholders, the local community where it operates, local businesses in that community, society at large (including future generations), the company's industry, and the business community at large. Behavior that benefits one constituency may well harm another one. So, socially responsible decision-making is a process, not a choice between obvious rights and wrongs, or as Gary describes it, "The real issue is commitment, intent, and then progress toward achieving your intent." Socially responsible businesses are those that make it their business to engage themselves in that process—unrelentingly.

## Toward a social bottom line

The mythology of American business grew out of the pioneering drive that established this nation—the self-made success story, the tough-minded manager who will accept nothing less than the achievement of a stated goal, the ingenuity of great inventors like Edison, Bell, and the Wright brothers. I find it at once ironic and, to say the least, contradictory for some business and government leaders first to trumpet their roots in our "can-do" business history, and then to shriek that economics and environmental preservation or economics and fair labor practices can't possibly be reconciled.

We find what we seek. More specifically, we predetermine our answers by the questions we ask. In the social arena, many of our existing problems seem to defy solutions because instead of asking ourselves the fundamental and unfettered question of how to solve them, we try to get away cheaply by asking what minor surgeries we can perform on the status quo.

For example, faced with smog-choked cities, clean-air mandates, and the prospect of outright bans of automotive traffic in some international cities, European and Japanese automakers are racing each other to develop the first environmentally viable passenger vehicle. The corporation that wins the race will be the one that asks the right question: How can we power an acceptably performing automobile without polluting at all?

America's automakers, seldom comfortable with fundamental research and development that would distract them from short-term goals, have entered the contest with one foot on the gas pedal and the other on the brake. Although faced with the prospect of severe clean-air mandates at home, they've approached the challenge by formulating the least challenging self-query possible: How can we preserve the infrastructure supporting our current meal ticket? They announced their answer in late 1993: Instead of emphasizing zero-emissions vehicles, they would modify existing technology to drop emissions by 70 percent within a decade. In addition, they would use this commitment to persuade states to adopt permissive clean-air standards that allow for their new vehicles.

Ultimately, this strategy is doomed to environmental failure because an increase in cars on the road or in miles driven per trip can overwhelm any pollution saved by tweaking the technology, just as happened with catalytic converters. By framing their search for an environmentally improved car in this unimaginative and socially unresponsive manner, our automakers have all but guaranteed that one of their competitors, not them, *will* solve the problem and patent it. Perhaps that competitor will be Mazda, which *has* asked the basic question and is now developing a hydrogen-powered Miata. If they are successful, they could well own the automobile future because the only by-product of hydrogen combustion is water.

The analogy—that fundamental questions asked unflinchingly can solve seemingly complex human problems—applies to management issues, too. For example, many executives wonder how they can get employees to act like partners in the company. Packagers Cin-Made Corporation (Cincinnati) and engine rebuilders Springfield Remanufacturing (Springfield, Missouri) asked the question without qualifying it and got the obvious answer—*make* employees partners through stock ownership plans or other financial incentives, teach them the things that partners need to know, and give them a say in company decisions. The new partners in turn produced spectacular results for the executives who empowered them.

Another question that many frustrated managers ask is, "Just what *do* employees want these days?" But few ask it of the employees themselves. At Stonyfield, management took the more direct route, and it's been a key to the company's outstanding performance. "We've had seven or eight benefits that we've implemented that have been what the employees asked for," Stonyfield's Gary Hirshberg notes. "That's been a big factor in our high morale, that employees say 'We want this' and they get it six months later. That's pretty rare in business, I think, but it's the alternative to our approach that doesn't make sense to me."

*The profit motive is not inherently wicked, but is rather a powerful engine that can be harnessed for virtually any purpose—including a socially responsible one.*

Business responsibility in general begins with such basic questions as: "How do we make a difference socially and still survive as a business?" and "How do we minimize our impact on the environment and still make a profit?" instead of the usual "How do we maximize profits this quarter and to hell with the fallout?" Many executives like Gary Hirshberg and many companies like Stonyfield appear to do everything wrong—diverting enormous portions of company resources and energy into social initiatives, investing in workers for the long haul, and ruling out all business opportunities predicated on social exploitation—because they're asking different sorts of questions. But they're still making money hand over fist—and proving, as *Business Ethics* magazine editor Marjorie Kelly puts it, "that the profit motive is not inherently wicked, but is rather a powerful engine that can be harnessed for virtually any purpose—including a socially responsible one."

The business advantages of orienting a company toward social responsibility hardly stop with creating more loyal and productive line employees and more devoted customers. In *Newsweek*, Stride Rite's Arnold

Hiatt noted how social responsibility also leads to a more sensitive management corps: "If you develop a certain acuity in listening to consumers, you also learn to listen well to your employees and to the community."

Hiatt's remarks speak to one of the essential, natural connections between social responsibility and profits. The company attuned to the needs of its customers, work force, and community also grows more in touch with shifts in the marketplace, culture, and its own internal functioning. Becoming more sensitive enables the company to do what all winning competitors do—that is, respond faster. This, not at all coincidentally, is also the literal definition of responsibility: response-ability, the ability to respond.

# 3
# Corporations Must Serve the Public Interest

### Ralph Estes

*A professor at American University in Washington, D.C., Ralph Estes is cofounder of the Center for Advancement of Public Policy. He is the au-thor of* Corporate Social Accounting, Accounting and Society, *and* Tyranny of the Bottom Line: Why Corporations Make Good People Do Bad Things.

Corporations in colonial America were originally given charters in order to serve the public good. However, the view that the corpo-rate charter serves the public interest has gradually been replaced by the belief that it serves the stockholders and the bottom line. A new accounting system—stakeholder accounting—should be used to measure corporations' performance toward employees, customers, local communities, and society at large. This system would allow corporate managers and communities to accurately assess a company's ethical record in these areas and provide man-agers with more incentive to make humane, socially responsible decisions.

The problem with our current system of accounting is that it is a biased scorekeeper. By accounting only for the return to shareholders, it pushes corporate managers to perform against one major goal, when in fact the typical corporation exists to achieve at least several goals. General Electric, for example, identifies about 10 goals, which include being a good employer, providing good products and services at a fair price, and being a good citizen. Typically, there is no accounting for any of these goals; the only thing we are able to judge readily is the profitability to shareholders.

Most importantly, there is no accounting for the major purpose for which the corporation exists. A corporation is not chartered by society to provide a return to stockholders. We allow that. But the reason we give corporations valuable charters is because we expect corporations to serve the public purpose.

Ralph Estes, "What You Count, You Get," *In Context*, no. 41, Summer 1995. Reprinted with permission.

The history of this is intriguing. Like other major changes that occur over a long period of time, this perversion of corporate purpose occurred gradually. When Queen Elizabeth I and her successors and subsequently the American colonies granted corporate charters, it was understood that serving the public was the reason for granting the special benefits contained in the charters.

Investors who invested in these corporations wanted an accounting for the investment—a perfectly reasonable desire, since the shareholders, more than other stakeholders, were often far removed from the operations of the corporation. So the stockholders hired auditors to *listen* for them, as the root of the word *auditor* suggests.

---

*The reason we give corporations valuable charters is because we expect corporations to serve the public purpose.*

---

As years went by, accountants kept on providing performance reports to the investors. But the sovereign and the state didn't keep asking for reports on how well the corporation was performing its public purpose. Employees, and until recently consumers, also failed to demand an accounting for how well corporations were performing for them. So we had a vacuum of accountability, and the only thing filling that vacuum was the accounting report to stockholders.

As a result, over the course of almost 300 years, we gradually turned from an understanding that the corporation is chartered to serve the public interest, toward a belief that it exists to serve stockholders and the bottom line.

## Costs and benefits

The new accounting system I'm proposing would report on how a corporation is serving its various constituents. Managers, who now make the decisions in contemplation of how they will look on that one-dimensional bottom line, would see that they are going to be held accountable for the cost to the other stakeholders as well. This would certainly affect their decisions.

I call this multi-dimensional system *stakeholder accounting*. Such a system would look much like the accounting income statement we have now, which has essentially one column that shows the revenues minus the expenses and the net—the bottom line. We should add about four sections—one for employees, one for customers, one for local communities, and one for the society at large. Each stakeholder's section or column would show the benefits that occur for these stakeholders, the costs inflicted on them, and their net result or "bottom line."

At the outset, much of this accounting will not be translated into dollars. What we need is information. We need a reporting of the layoff record of a company so that workers can make informed employment decisions. We need a detailed reporting of statistics on hiring, placement, and promotion of women and minorities, so that women and minorities contemplating moving from one firm to another can assess their prospects. We need a reporting of the emissions, the toxic substances stored on site, the hazardous waste created in the community.

It's not difficult to implement such a system; the first step is a very easy one. A corporation that wants to be accountable to its stakeholders need only make accessible to all the information it presently collects and files with various federal agencies. Right now, workers don't have access to the corporation's EEOC (Equal Employment Opportunity Commission) filings, for example. As a result, the people who are most affected by whether the corporation is discriminating are unable to judge for themselves whether they are going into an environment that is discriminatory.

Likewise with communities asked to provide tax breaks to corporations that promise to create jobs—what is the company's actual job creation record in other communities that have given it favors? Or how many injuries, of what type and magnitude, have occurred in the department and workstation a potential employee would be joining? The company has ready access to the data in its files; the worker needs this information to make an informed labor market decision.

## Reporting to the public

Imagine that the corporate reports for all the corporations in your city or town are released each year by March 31. These are filed with the Corporate Accountability Commission (formerly the SEC [Securities and Exchange Commission]) and also kept on file at the city clerk's office, the labor district offices, and at corporate headquarters. The news media jumps on this information just like they do now when the annual stockholders' report comes out. On the nightly business report, we have a detailed comparison of the pollution of all of the large corporations located in your city, and how their environmental performance has changed over the last year. The media seeks interviews with the CEOs and environmental protection officers of these corporations to get explanations of any changes in pollution levels.

A worker, a city council member, a member of Congress, anyone who wants to know what the corporation is doing in these important areas can get information simply by reading this annual corporate report.

---

*We gradually turned from an understanding that the corporation is chartered to serve the public interest, toward a belief that it exists to serve stockholders and the bottom line.*

---

With this kind of information public, managers would have good reason to make different decisions—it would be a different and a more responsible corporate America. And in fact, it would be one that corporate managers would rather work in, because it would free them to be as good as they want to be, instead of being bound to the tyranny of the bottom line.

We've got to remember that what these managers sometimes do is evil, but they aren't evil people. They learned to accept the standards of a system that says this: If you are faced with a question of closing a plant in Dodge City, Kansas, that will put 5,000 people out of work and devastate a community, devastate a school system, devastate a police department, devastate the social fabric of that community, leaving many of these people never to work again, in order to move that plant to Juarez, Mexico, to earn a 0.5 percent higher return on investment for the stockholders and a few pennies more in earnings per share, then you've got to do it. You can feel sorry for Dodge City, but you've got to do it. Managers don't like to do that, but they do it because the bottom line forces them to.

There are examples of companies trying to swim upstream against the tide and serve the needs and the interests of the whole set of stakeholders. But that inexorable pressure of the bottom line keeps drawing them back, and as soon as one CEO leaves, or as soon as times get a bit hard, they fall back on the same kind of behavior they were engaging in in the past.

By changing the accounting system and the accountability system, managers will be able to make more humane, more socially responsible decisions consistently, and will benefit from doing so.

# Corporations Should Be Philanthropic

## Bill Shaw and Frederick R. Post

*Bill Shaw is the Woodson Centennial Professor in Business Adminis-tration at the University of Texas in Austin. Frederick R. Post is an as-sistant professor of business law and management at the University of Toledo in Ohio. They have both written articles for law and business ethics journals.*

Many businesses are philanthropic strictly for their own self-interest; their donations reflect positively on the firm's image and reputation. However, there are moral reasons for a company to give to the community. Because corporate giving benefits both the corporation and the community, it is consistent with the phi-losophy of utilitarianism, which seeks the greatest good for the greatest number. Other reasons for corporate giving include the increasing depersonalization of corporate ownership, legal prece-dents allowing corporate directors to consider interests other than those of their shareholders, and the inability of the government to meet all of society's needs.

Discussions of corporate social responsibility invariably include a de-bate over corporate philanthropic efforts. Is corporate philanthropy simply a public relations ploy, a purely egoistic endeavor, or does it have a compelling moral justification? Few would dispute the social value of corporate support for community and cultural projects, projects ranging from the purchase of school band uniforms to the financial backing of the New York Metropolitan Opera. These and other worthwhile endeav-ors often are not financially self-sustaining, and the tradition of corporate giving has long kept many of them afloat.

The reason for the moral limbo of corporate philanthropy is particu-larly glaring. Corporate giving is an extension of personal giving, but there is an important difference—it is roughly the difference between you giving away your money and you giving away mine (Friedman, 1970). This is where the issue is joined. Given the separation of ownership and

Bill Shaw and Frederick R. Post, "A Moral Basis for Corporate Philanthropy," *Journal of Business Ethics*, vol. 12 (October 1993), pp. 745–51; ©1993 Kluwer Academic Publishers. Reprinted with permission.

control in the large, publicly held modern corporation, decisions about corporate policies are made by those who are not the owners (Berle and Means). It follows, then, that if corporate giving has no sounder moral foundation than the personal agenda of the board chairman or the CEO, such programs will always be suspect and always under attack. Since corporate philanthropy advances our cultural quality of life so enormously, we think that it is important to articulate a moral basis that will sustain it, nurture its growth, and move it beyond the realm of a thinly disguised public relations activity.

*If corporate giving has no sounder moral foundation than the personal agenda of the board chairman or the CEO, such programs will always be suspect.*

On the other hand, we do not regard it as ignoble that community and cultural programs financed by corporate revenues reflect positively upon the image, reputation, and goodwill of the firm The motivations for such projects seem to us to be an amalgam of altruism, good citizenship, prudence, and sound investment strategy. These are motivations that owners, managers, and the corporate workforce share. They are honorable motives, and the element of self-interest is in need of no apology.

In this viewpoint, however, we argue that the moral basis for corporate giving is more compelling than ethical egoism. Ethical egoism, of course, takes the "self" as the center of the universe. It evaluates all options on their relative payoffs to the self, that is, on the degree to which the options maximize the interests of the "player," the egoist. All other consequences are irrelevant to the decision. This is not to say that the ethical egoist will not factor in the interests of others, but, on those occasions, advancing the interests of others is never the primary objective. Others are simply means to the end of maximizing the ethical egoist's advantage.

Utilitarianism, like ethical egoism, is teleological in structure. Its purpose or objective, i.e., its *telos*, is popularly characterized as "the greatest good for the greatest number." In concept, utilitarianism envisions the aggregation or summation of individual utilities. These utilities are variously described—hedonists view them in terms of physical pleasure/pain while other utilitarians view them qualitatively.

We are inclined toward the qualitative assessment of J.S. Mill, "better to be a Socrates dissatisfied, than a pig satisfied." Despite its computational and other pitfalls, for purposes of this viewpoint, we advance Mill's view. On our best understanding of his position, we will proceed to make our arguments in support of corporate giving.

In doing so, we want to make clear our view that other ethical traditions supply an equally compelling foundation for corporate giving. This is particularly true of virtue ethics. Not by any means do we suggest an identity of these teleological theories, but with regard to the matter at hand we do acknowledge some kinship. In virtue ethics, at least in the Aristotelean tradition, the good for man was to be sought in a community or *polis* that recognized and honored such character traits (virtues) as liberality, magnificence, and pride. In the U.S. today we would likely render those "propensities to excellence" somewhat differently, e.g., public spiritedness, generosity, compassion. But, in keeping with that tradition, the virtues would define the ideals of what we mean by "good character." (Solomon, 1992)

While Athens, the *polis* of Aristotle's age, did not embody an economy driven by anything like the modern corporation, it did esteem excellence in character, and it trained its young citizens to link their personal well-being with the good of the community. This surely gives us a reason for supposing that virtuous people would expect their institutions, i.e., their corporations and the people who manage them, to foster "the good."

With regard to the practice of philanthropy, in this case corporate philanthropy, we could assume that it would be undertaken with prudence, which is to say neither excessively nor stingily but with the objective of advancing the corporate good and the good of the whole. With this aside, we are only attempting to document our view that other ethical traditions, even traditions with no kinship to either virtue ethics or utility, may be found equally supportive of the concept of corporate giving.

## The stockholders' obligation

Putting aside for now any further consideration of the other traditions and returning to our focus on utilitarianism, we argue that corporate stockholders in their role as stockholders, and in their role as members of the social community, share with all others the obligation to act, or to follow a rule governing a class of acts, that will maximize the public welfare. Further, these stockholders have every reason to expect corporate officers to obey the law and equally good reason to expect corporate officers to advance the public welfare in the exercise of their practical business judgments. It is beyond question that the law permits corporate officials this measure of discretion.[1] The use of corporate funds, then, to support quality-of-life, community projects is consistent with the law and with ethical theory.

In Section II we discuss some of the contemporary criticisms of corporate giving and respond to them from a utilitarian perspective. We summarize recent empirical research supporting a view widely shared by business executives, and the view we advance in this viewpoint, that corporations should have an expanded citizenship role. The marketing and educational efforts of nonpublic, philanthropic institutions give additional evidence of the widely accepted view that corporations do have a moral duty to advance the public welfare.

In Section III we describe how the changed structure of U.S. corporations has transferred greater power and responsibility into the hands of management (Berle and Means, 1932). This monumental structural shift—the separation of ownership from control—has resulted in correspondingly less power and involvement by shareholders. Next we advance the position that the capitalist market morality presupposes a rule utilitarian world-view that fosters trust, fairness, loyalty, respect for the well-being of community members, and generally minimizes harm in the process of promoting the public good. We find rule utilitarianism to be harmonious with and to support the on-going efforts of the business community to develop and maintain lasting relationships with corporate stakeholders. These objectives are neither achievable nor sustainable through immoral conduct such as deception, lying, breach of trust, bad faith and the like. Finally, we argue that our moral justification of corporate giving is supplemented by social forces including trends in the law, practical judgments, and by contemporary economic conditions in an increasingly competitive global marketplace.

## II. Corporate giving: theft or moral mandate?

Corporate giving, as an aspect of corporate social responsibility, has been criticized by Milton Friedman as roughly the equivalent of theft. At the very least it amounts to "spending someone else's money" to solve social problems—problems that the corporation did not cause and problems that are normally understood to be in the legislative or political domain. He further argues that corporate managers operate under a moral mandate to "make as much money for the stockholders as they can within the limits of the law and ethical custom" (Friedman, 1970). The diversion of corporate resources to community programs, then, he equates with waste and with a breach of fiduciary duty.

It nevertheless appears that Friedman invites all but the most extravagant and most foolish corporate-community endeavors. For example, he does not find these projects to be objectionable if there is some degree of positive economic feedback to the firm. Hence, Friedman endorses corporate spending on community amenities such as parks and playgrounds if that contributes to employee morale or enhances employee loyalty to the firm with the consequence of greater employee pride, cohesion, and quality of workmanship. In other words, if within the rational business judgment of management, corporate involvement and the commitment of corporate resources to community projects reflects favorably on the "bottom line," or has the potential to do so, it escapes his condemnation of wastefulness and disloyalty. Hence, Friedman endorses corporate philanthropic endeavors as long as they are based upon strategic considerations. Under this approach, policy choices must be guided by long-term corporate objectives, and, within that framework, management must exercise its best judgment as to how widely to open the door to corporate philanthropy. Legally, management's largess is curtailed only by the boundary of "gross negligence," and that is a boundary to which Friedman voices no objection.

What kind of moral worth can be attributed to such endeavors, if any at all? We take the Friedman position to articulate some version of ethical egoism—or, at best, a grudging variety of enlightened self-interest. If it is not essentially devoid of any real concern for the welfare of others (except, of course, shareholders), it diminishes the value of others to the level of mere instruments. To phrase the matter differently, others are to be served just well enough to deliver a satisfactory return to the shareholders. In keeping with this view, Friedman sees it as the role of law to prevent employees and others from being blatantly exploited, and also the role of law, rather than the role of the corporation, to combat social evils.

We want to make plain our view that self-interest, particularly the self-interest component implicit in corporate giving, is not incompatible with a morally compelling justification for corporate giving. But, while

Friedman instructs us that ethical egoism, coupled with a limited degree of government intervention, is a sufficient moral framework for our nation's corporate establishment, we find this framework to be far too limiting. Further, we believe that Friedman's views, presented more than twenty years ago, are not in step with the role that is expected of corporate management today. It seems equally clear that Friedman has failed to provide substance to his call for the observance of "ethical custom." While the phrase "ethical custom" bristles with potential, in his hands it languishes in disuse. It has become an empty term that belittles the call of a society's moral sensibility. Given the change in corporate structure, that is, the transfer of corporate power from owners to managers, it is essential that corporate management, acting for the collective moral conscience of the corporate stakeholders, seize the leadership in advancing "the greatest good for the greatest number."

The utilitarian focus of corporate executives has recently been demonstrated in an empirical fashion. In a survey of member companies conducted by the Business Committee for the Arts, executives were asked why they participated in corporate philanthropy (Vartorella, 1992). The overwhelmingly dominant response of executives was corporate citizenship (91%), followed by enhancing image (65%), media coverage (35%), production promotion (28%), and increasing sales (20%). This evidence of utilitarian support for corporate philanthropy—evidence which, by the way, is not inconsistent with virtue ethics or with deontological moral theory—edges image enhancement (which we identity principally with egoism) by a significant margin.

Nonprofit, charitable institutions seeking funding from the private sector demonstrate a clear understanding of corporate citizenship. In fact, institutional and industry newsletters—including the Corporate Philanthropy Report,[2] the Chronicle of Philanthropy,[3] and the Fund Raising Institute Monthly Portfolio[4]—place heavy emphasis upon the social and ethical obligations of private industry. Seminars which the consulting industry designs to educate nonprofits about fundraising opportunities also emphasize the need to address these obligations.[5] Corporate executives seem most favorably disposed to act upon philanthropic requests that reflect contemporary perceptions of the duty of the corporation to the community to be a good corporate citizen.

## III. The changed role of the shareholder owner

Recent research into the internal structure of the American corporation asserts that a variety of forces have conjoined to diminish the traditional ownership role of the shareholder in the American corporation (Nesteruk, 1989). While corporate law describes shareholders as the owners, there has been a transition from "owners" to "investors" and then again to simple "beneficiaries." Further, because the law has recognized corporate legal status as that of a separate and distinct person (an artificial or legal person) and because of the fact that a corporation can only act through its agents or managers, other structural realities follow. The management group must have considerable discretion and power to effectuate the actions of this artificial person, and with this discretion and power goes moral responsibility for its exercise (Nesteruk, 1990).

We are in agreement with this analysis, which also notes that the transition has both distorted and practically eliminated shareholder ability to influence corporate policy. This places even greater responsibility on corporate management to exercise moral responsibility on behalf of the shareholders who have now become simply the beneficiaries of corporate policies. "The central thrust of corporate social responsibility (is) summoning management to exhibit a concern for the social good through its assumption of a new role, that of corporate good citizen" (Nesteruk, 1989).

This phenomenon in the modern corporation is described as a disaggregation of ownership. The disaggregation can be divided into three stages: traditional ownership, corporate ownership, and beneficiary ownership. Traditional ownership entails control over property. In a small closely held corporation, shareholders do exercise control, but as the corporation becomes larger and hires professional managers, as is typically done in the large publicly held corporation, traditional ownership disappears and there is a separation of control from ownership. This was observed and documented years ago by Berle and Means in their seminal treatise on American corporations (Berle and Means, 1932).

*Self-interest, particularly the self-interest component implicit in corporate giving, is not incompatible with a morally compelling justification for corporate giving.*

As the role of owner changes from owner to investor, there is a depersonalization of the shareholders' relation to the corporation. With this depersonalization, the concern of the shareholder shifts myopically from traditional broad ownership concerns to a single goal—higher profit. The increasing dominance of institutional investors such as mutual funds, pension plans, and money managers has signaled further change. The ownership role of the shareholder has now become even more remote. It has reached the point where shareholders can be characterized as mere beneficiaries of the results of corporate success—beneficiaries who have no real input or impact upon corporate decision-making.

For management to consider the interests of constituencies other than shareholders is not without legal precedent. With regard to whom the corporation should serve, a question posed within the context of the takeover phenomenon in the 1980's, one commentator observed that there has been "the adoption by, at last count, about 30 states of so-called 'other constituency' statutes which, in one form or another, purport to permit or require directors to consider the interests of other groups in addition to shareholders in making their decisions" (Sommer, 1991). For example, the corporate statute in Ohio specifically provides that, in addition to traditional shareholder interests, the directors "may consider . . . the economy of the state and nation, and *community and societal considerations*" (emphasis added) (Sommer, 1991). Thus, our argument for a utilitarian-based justification for corporate giving does not conflict with the statutory law prevailing in a majority of the states.

Another legal commentator, arguing for language in the American

Law Institute's Corporate Governance Project that would mandate the integration of ethical considerations into business conduct and require the commitment of a "reasonable amount" of corporate resources to public welfare, humanitarian, educational, philanthropic purposes,[6] defends his position as follows:

> Government, burdened by continuing deficits, unfortunately lacks the resources to effectively address many pressing national concerns. Private individual efforts also fall short of the needs. Large corporations, on the other hand, are the dominant institutions in our economy and in that sphere are amazingly efficient organizations. Much of the nation's wealth lies in their treasuries. For both pragmatic and theoretical reasons, the law should require that they broaden their mission to promote the common welfare as well as their own profitability (Morrissey, 1989).

This writer boldly proposes that philanthropy should not only be encouraged but legally required. While we question the feasibility of such a legal mandate, the publication of such a view in a respected legal journal evidences an acknowledgement within the legal literature that corporations must do more in a time of restricted and declining governmental resources.

After reviewing several well-publicized examples of corporate philanthropy and summarizing the views of recent court decisions that have both sanctioned and promoted such corporate action, a third legal commentator concluded that "[t]wo propositions seem valid: (1) any gift can be couched in such terms (enhancing the overall good will of the corporation by improving the corporation's reputation and promoting favorable public attitudes toward it) as to promise the kinds of intangible, long-run benefits held by the courts as legally sufficient; and (2) any charitable contribution to the generally recognized social causes thus benefits the corporation" (Green, 1990). This is certainly consistent with our view regarding the need for U.S. firms to assume broader moral responsibilities. This assumption of responsibility, we will show, is not incompatible with the capitalist market mentality and morality—both of which rest upon the continuing exercise of fundamental moral commitments.

## IV. Capitalist market morality

On at least two occasions, Friedman addresses the moral basis for managerial conduct. Within the context of his familiar admonition to obey the law while maximizing shareholder return, he relates that managers should be guided by "ethical custom" (Friedman, 1970), and should engage in "full and fair competition without deception or fraud" (Friedman, 1962). In addressing the moral tone of business, he is describing the prevailing capitalist market mentality—our market system must operate on trust to be successful during any long-term relationship. For example, common sense indicates that developing the kind of relationship that is necessary in business would be impossible unless truth-telling was the norm. If there was no trust in a business handshake, if good faith could not be placed in the written and spoken word, the system would degenerate quickly into chaos. If express and implied promises were not kept, if employees, suppliers, and customers were not treated fairly, and if business firms did not refrain from actions that foreseeably inflicted injury on their customers and the community, the system could not survive. Conduct of that description would violate the internal moral structure, the moral coherence, of the capitalist system.

Most businesses not only survive but thrive by developing repeat business within their industry. Observing the moral injunctions of honesty, fairness, truth-telling and the like are essential for lasting, long-term business relationships. As a rule, these behaviors advance the greatest benefit for the greatest number, namely, those whose well-being is affected by the corporation: customers, suppliers, the community, the shareholders, the employees, and the managers. Projection of the opposite traits—lying, breach of trust, bad faith—is counterproductive. It produces only short-term gains and destroys the hope for productive relationships. Such practices are not the kinds of behaviors that we invite others to apply in their dealings with us, and, as a rule, these behaviors do not produce the "greatest good for the greatest number."

---

*For management to consider the interests of constituencies other than shareholders is not without legal precedent.*

---

Corporate management would, however, be well advised to observe a note of caution prior to any commitments to support community projects that attack social ills such as poverty, hunger and homelessness. These are problems that have not been caused by corporate conduct and presumably the corporation will not be particularly expert in resolving them. As Friedman has argued, these are problems that we normally delegate to our democratic institutions. There is no reason to suppose, however, that corporate and other private efforts cannot make some positive contribution to people in need even if that contribution is short-term and relatively minor compared to the magnitude of the task. The choice should not be posed as "all or nothing"—there is an ample middle ground. To the extent that corporate time, talent, and resources are available, corporate management should weigh these capabilities against the community need and, on appropriate occasions, go to the "rescue." If, in contrast, the corporation has actually caused the harm through environmental pollution, unsafe working conditions, or some other direct action, then the moral duty for direct corporate "rescue" is clearly evident.

The extent of the causal link provides a litmus test of the extent of moral responsibility. If there is no causal link to any prior corporate action, then the moral obligation to provide money to solve the problem, particularly one far distanced from corporate expertise and one that is normally on the political agenda, is certainly less compelling. Such decision-making by corporate management is analogous to that practiced in our personal lives. As a rule, most of us do not spend ourselves into bankruptcy by rushing out to the rescue of the homeless, the minority college fund, or the local symphony. And if we do not do these things with our own money, the argument that corporate managers should do it with "someone else's money" is even less persuasive.

Rescue obligations, then, are clearly in need of some mediating considerations (Simon *et al.*, 1972). We believe that such guidelines can be determined by identifying the "ethical custom" or the "ethical culture" of our society. No one would expect a nonswimmer to jump off of a bridge to save a drowning man. Neither is it expected of corporate managers in their role of exercising "reasonable business judgment" to waste lives or resources on futile projects. But, having consulted the available corporate resources, i.e., the firm's time, talent, and financial capacity for doing good, and having balanced those resources against the magnitude of the social need, there may well be an obligation to go to the rescue.

## V. Self-interest and utilitarianism

Business in the corporate form is not an identity separate and apart from the society that charters its existence and nurtures its success. The connection between business and its many social constituencies is, foremost, a moral connection. While there are individuals and corporations engaging in philanthropic efforts based exclusively on ethical egoism, we believe that a more compelling and morally fulfilling justification exists. While there is a proper role for self-interest, it is a role that is not paramount or "trumps." Our effort has been to show that self-interest is not always in opposition to "the greatest good for the greatest number" because the giver is a member of the community that reaps the reward. When there is an irreconcilable opposition between self-interest and utility, however, the good of the whole prevails. Finally the restructured relationships within the modern, publicly held corporation, the liberalization of most state corporate statutory frameworks, and the inability of overburdened governmental resources to meet many of society's most pressing needs, all reinforce the necessity for an expanded justification for an expanded commitment to corporate giving.

## *Notes*

1. Officers and directors are entitled to the presumption that "in making a business decision, the directors of a corporation acted on an informed basis, in good faith and in the honest belief that the action was taken in the best interest of the company." Aronson v. Lewis, 473 A.2d 805, 812 (Del. 1984). Unless these officers or directors have engaged in some fraud upon the company, or have acted with a conflict of interest, a court will hold them liable only for their "gross negligence." Smith v. Van Gorkom, 488 A.2d 858, 873 (Del. 1985).

2. The Corporate Philanthropy Report (CPR) is a monthly newsletter which provides news and views concerning corporate citizenship practices of corporations around the world. Many major U.S. corporations and most nonprofits subscribe to the newsletter. In addition to being a source of information through the monthly newsletter, CPR has sponsored significant conferences and seminars which provide unique opportunities for intellectual exchange and networking. Examples of such conferences include the 1991 Japan at the American Grassroots series and the 1988 Media and Philanthropy conference. The address of CPR is 2727 Fairview Avenue East, Suite G, Seattle, WA 98102.

3. The Chronicle of Philanthropy is a biweekly newsletter which provides current information on philanthropy such as statistical analysis, donor profiles, and sources for new grants. The address is 1225 23rd St. NW, Washington, DC 20037.

4. The Fund Raising Institute Monthly Portfolio (FRI) is a monthly newsletter devoted to philanthropy which contains excerpts of relevant studies and articles discussing the latest trends in corporate philanthropy. The institute may be contacted at 12300 Twinbrook Parkway, Suite 450, Rockville, MD 20852.

5. As an example of how diverse such promotion efforts have become, in 1992 CPR is co-hosting a series of workshops emphasizing Asian philanthropy. The sessions are being marketed through promotional literature that describes them as being "geared toward those who already know the basics of fund raising but wish to know the particulars about this newly emerging source of support." The Workshops are touted as being able to "give you the tools you need to develop ties with Asian donors."

6. The American Law Institute (ALI) in its recent Corporate Governance Project has developed a series of drafts containing position statements on the role of the modern corporation. In Section 2.01, "The Objective and Conduct of the Business Corporation," the draft expands corporate purpose beyond that of just making profits for the shareholders. The expanded purpose included language in subsection (b) that the corporation "may take into account ethical considerations that are reasonably regarded as appropriate to the responsible conduct of business, and (c) may devote a reasonable amount of resources to public welfare, humanitarian, educational, and philanthropic purposes."

## References

Berle, A. and G. Means: 1932, *The Modern Corporation and Private Property* (Macmillan, New York).

Friedman, M.: 1970, 'The Social Responsibility of Business Is to Increase Its Profits,' *New York Times Magazine* 32, 13 Sept., 122–126.

Friedman, M.: 1962, *Capitalism and Freedom* (Free Press, New York).

Green, S.: 1990, 'Corporate Philanthropy and the Business Benefit: The Need for Clarity', *Golden Gate University Law Review* **20**, 239–260.

Mill, J.S.: 1989, *On Liberty; With the Subjection of Women; and Chapters on Socialism* (Cambridge University Press, New York).

Morrissey, D.: 1989, 'Toward a New/Old Theory of Corporate Social Responsibility', *Syracuse Law Review* **40**, 1005–1039.

Nesteruk, J.: 1990, 'Persons, Property, and the Corporation: A Proposal for a New Paradigm', *DePaul Law Review* **39**, 543–565.

Nesteruk, J.: 1989, 'Corporations, Shareholders, and Moral Choice: A New Perspective on Corporate Social Responsibility', *Cincinnati Law Review* **58**, 451–475.

Simon, J., C. Powers and J. Gunnemann: 1972, *The Ethical Investor: Universities and Corporate Responsibility* (Yale University Press, New Haven).

Solomon, R.: 1992, 'Corporate Roles, Personal Virtues: An Aristotelean Approach to Business Ethics', *Business Ethics Quarterly* 2, 317–340.

Sommer, Jr., A.: 1991, 'Whom Should the Corporation Serve? The Berle–Dodd Debate Revised Sixty Years Later', *Delaware Journal of Corporate Law* **16**, 33–56.

Vartorella, W.: 1992, 'Playing the Corporate Game: An Insider's Guide to Getting Equipment Grants', *Fund Raising Institute Monthly Portfolio* 31(7), 1–2.

# 5

# Many Multinational Businesses Are Not Socially Responsible

## Joseph LaDou

*Joseph LaDou is chief of the Division of Occupational and Environmental Medicine at the University of California, San Francisco. As a director of the International Commission on Occupational Health, he has investigated working conditions in newly industrialized countries.*

Many First World corporations have moved their operations to Mexico or Third World countries where wages are low and regulations on pollution and hazardous waste are lax or nonexistent. In addition, these multinational companies often maintain a double standard regarding worker health and safety regulations; at home in the United States or Europe they comply rigorously with safety standards, but overseas they let the standards fall to the levels of less developed nations. These poor host countries may reap the benefits of new jobs and investment, but they are at risk for major industrial accidents. Industrialized countries should insist that multinational corporations adhere to the same regulations abroad as they do at home.

In 1988, a California manufacturer of epoxy coating materials decided that it could no longer afford to make its products in the United States. The cost of complying with new emission standards for the solvents the products contained would simply have been too high. Yet the company learned that if it set up shop in Mexico, it not only could use the same solvents but could dump waste solvents at no cost into the arroyo behind the plant.

It's no secret that the low cost of manufacturing in Third World and newly industrialized countries has prompted thousands of First World corporations and investment groups to set up manufacturing operations there. The biggest lure, of course, is cheap labor—factory wages in countries such as Thailand, Bangladesh, Ghana, Guatemala, and Bolivia are of-

Joseph LaDou, "Deadly Migration," *Technology Review*, July 1991. Reprinted with permission from *Technology Review*, ©1991.

ten as low as 5 percent of those in industrialized countries. Companies also manufacture abroad to be closer to foreign markets and to overcome trade barriers. In return, the host countries reap significant benefits. According to the U.N. Environment Programme, foreign companies and investors have provided 60 percent of all industrial investment in developing countries over the past decade. For many nations, such investment is the primary source of new jobs.

*More and more manufacturers are moving their hazardous and polluting operations to less developed countries.*

But the industrial migration has a perverse side, the extent of which the California epoxy case can barely hint at. As developed nations enact laws promoting environmental and occupational safety, more and more manufacturers are moving their hazardous and polluting operations to less developed countries, most of which have either no environmental and worker-safety regulations or little power to enforce those that are on the books. Hazardous industries have migrated to many parts of Africa, Asia, and Eastern Europe. Japan, for example, with its limited land and dense population, has a pressing need to export manufacturing industries such as electronics, chemical production, and metal refining. And many European nations have exported hazardous industries such as textiles, petrochemicals, mining, and smelting.

There is an ironic twist to the problem. Countries that spend little on things like sewage systems, water treatment plants, and enforcement of environmental and occupational safety can offer tax rates dramatically lower than those in the industrialized world. Foreign-based manufacturers take the bait and move in, polluting waterways and endangering workers. Yet the host government can't afford remedies because of the low tax rate.

Pollution and working conditions are so bad that, in effect, the Industrial Revolution is taking place all over again, but with much larger populations of workers and in many more countries. And many of the resulting deaths and injuries are taking place with the complicity of First World companies.

## The faces of exploitation

The practice of using less developed nations as a dumping ground for untreated factory waste is but one of many forms the export of industrial hazards can take. Industries whose markets in developed countries are shrinking because of environmental concerns are vigorously promoting their products in the less health-conscious Third World. DDT is a compelling example. Its worldwide production, led by U.S. and European companies, is at record levels, even though it has been illegal to produce or use the pesticide in the United States and Europe since the 1970s.

Asbestos is another distressing example. To stimulate the development of companies that will produce asbestos products, Canada's government sends free samples of the material to a number of poorer countries, where many workers and communities are still unaware of the mineral's dangers. (Bangladesh received 790 tons, worth $600,000, in 1984.) Partly as a result of such promotion, Canadian asbestos exports to South Korea increased from 5,000 tons in 1980 to 44,000 tons in 1989. Exports to Pakistan climbed from 300 tons to 6,000 tons in the same period. Canada now exports close to half its asbestos to the Third World.

The First World also exports entire industries—including most lead smelting, refining, and product manufacture—that present occupational hazards. In developed nations, companies using processes that involve lead are required to take costly precautions to protect workers. U.S. lead workers must receive special training, have proper work clothes and changing facilities, and go on paid leave if tests reveal high lead levels in the blood. But in the lax regulator climate of Malaysia, most lead-acid battery workers—at both foreign- and locally owned plants—have lead levels three times locally owned plants—have lead levels three times as high as allowed in U.S. workers. And lead plants exported to India continue operating even though 10 percent of the workers have lead poisoning.

Even a migrating industry that doesn't involve toxic materials can be hazardous, because First World corporations often apply a double standard to worker safety. At home, they might comply rigorously with health and safety regulations. Abroad, the same companies let safety standards plummet to the levels prevailing in the less developed host country.

Those levels are miserably low. Worker fatality rates are at least twice as high in industrializing countries, and workplace injuries occur with a frequency not seen in the developed nations since the early years of the Industrial Revolution. Workers in poor countries—usually with limited education, skill, and training—tend to labor in small, crowded factories with old, unsafe machinery, dangerous noise levels, and unsound buildings. Protective gear is seldom available. The companies also tend to be geographically scattered and inaccessible to health and safety inspectors.

On learning of such conditions in India or Malaysia, we in the First World may wince but may also be tempted to put them out of mind—to regard them as a Third World problem from which we are comfortably remote. Yet Americans need look no farther than their own southern border to find some of the worst instances of migrating industries' disregard for human health and environmental safety. Many of the factories that U.S. and other foreign interests operate in northern Mexico freely pollute the water, the air, and the ground and subject workers to conditions nothing short of Dickensian.

## The siesta of reason

In 1965, Mexico sought to overcome chronic unemployment through the Border Industrialization Program, designed to lure foreign manufacturing business—mainly from the United States—into Mexican border states. The country's government hoped that foreign capital would flow into the economy along with modern production methods that would help create a skilled workforce.

Under the program, manufacturers send raw materials and equipment to Mexico. If they agree to take back the finished products, they need pay taxes only on the value added in Mexico instead of on the value of the entire product. Another big draw is that factory wages average about $5.40 per nine-hour day, less than in Korea, Taiwan, Hong Kong, and other countries long favored for off-shore manufacturing. For U.S. investors, the cost of transporting goods and materials to and from northern Mexico is lower as well.

Today, nearly 1,800 factories operate under this program in northern Mexico, employing about half a million workers. The plants, known as "maquiladoras," extend from Tijuana in the west to Matamoros on the Gulf of Mexico. Their owners include some of the largest U.S. corporations: IBM, General Electric, Motorola, Ford, Chrysler, General Motors, RCA, United Technologies, ITT, Eastman Kodak, and Zenith. Japan's Sony, Matsushita, Hitachi, Yazaki, and TDK also run maquiladoras, as do numerous European companies.

Most maquiladoras are small plants with fewer than 100 workers. In the program's early years, they were largely clothing manufacturers and hand assembly operations, employing mostly women. Today maquiladoras manufacture or assemble a wide range of products, from automobile parts to high-technology electronic components. Men now account for close to 40 percent of the workforce.

*Many of the factories that U.S. and other foreign interests operate in northern Mexico freely pollute the water, the air, and the ground.*

No one disputes that the main goal of the Border Industrialization Program has been met. The estimated $3 billion in foreign exchange earnings that maquiladoras pump into the Mexican economy each year now exceeds revenues from tourism and is second only to Mexico's oil and gas exports. Virtually all the new manufacturing jobs created in Mexico in the past decade—and a fifth of the country's manufacturing jobs overall—resulted from the rapid growth of the maquiladoras.

Yet these benefits have come at a high cost. The Border Industrialization Program has created serious social and environmental problems in both countries, but especially in Mexico. The prospect of employment in maquiladoras has caused the populations of border towns and cities to swell. Since 1970, for example, Nogales (south of Tucson) has grown fourfold to 250,000, and Juarez (across the Rio Grande from El Paso) has grown from 250,000 to 1.5 million.

Overcrowding strains these municipalities beyond their limits. Tens of thousands of workers subsist in cardboard huts in squatters' camps without heat or electricity, and sewage is dumped into the arroyos, through which it flows to the nearest river or estuary. At least 10 million gallons of raw sewage from Mexico flows into the Tijuana River every day, polluting San Diego's beaches. The Mexican government is so hard pressed to deal with the problem that the U.S. government, the state of California, and the city of San Diego have agreed to pay most of the $192 million cost of a treatment plant on the border.

But maquiladoras do more than just overburden sewers. Many owners and managers—especially of small maquiladoras engaged in metal

48 At Issue

working, plating, printing, tanning, and dyeing—readily admit that they moved their operations to Mexico partly because hazardous processes are unwelcome in the United States and other developed countries, and that Mexico is not creating any serious obstacle to their activities. As one owner of a furniture factory explained to me, "I can find lots of Mexican workers in the United States. What I can't find here in Tijuana is the government looking over my shoulder."

---

*Foreign operators have little incentive to make sure the 20 million tons of hazardous waste that maquiladoras generate each year is properly disposed of.*

---

Indeed, the very terms of the Border Industrialization Program seem to encourage recklessness. Many foreign companies or investment groups set up maquiladoras through the Mexican government's "shelter program," whereby the parent company—typically known only to the government—maintains control of production and a Mexican company forms to act as co-manager. This shelter firm recruits, trains, and pays all the Mexicans in the workforce. It also manages relationships with the local community and with the Mexican government. In short, foreigners run the business while their Mexican partners see to the social tasks. Because it is a Mexican corporation, the shelter operator shields the foreign company from liability in case Mexico ever cracks down on violators.

Consequently, the foreign operators have little incentive to make sure the 20 million tons of hazardous waste that maquiladoras generate each year is properly disposed of. No data are available on how much of this waste is deposited in rivers and streams, the air, or the ground, but the volumes are enormous. For example, the New River flows northward from Baja California into California contaminated by industrial wastes such as chloroform, benzene, toluene, zylene, and PCBs, and by agricultural runoff that contains various pesticides, including DDT. The river also carries more than 20 million gallons of raw sewage each day.

California has evaluated numerous alternatives to protect community health and Imperial Valley agriculture. The cheapest solution is to provide the Mexican city of Mexicali with a wastewater collection and treatment system, following the approach proposed for Tijuana sewage. The U.S. Environmental Protection Agency may eventually have to take similar action for all the major cities and towns along the U.S.-Mexico border. In that event, the U.S. taxpayer would ultimately pay for the reduced cost to industry of manufacturing in Mexico.

Mexico's lax monitoring of industrial practices encourages dumping of hazardous waste. Under Mexican law, toxic materials brought in by plants for use in manufacturing—such as paints, cleaning solvents, oils, and acids—must be returned to the country of origin or recycled in Mexico. But according to the Texas Water Commission, only about 60 percent of these waste materials leave Mexico. The other 40 percent—much of it toxic, the commission reports—is disposed of illegally in Mexico's sewers, drainage systems, and landfills. When waste is returned to the

United States, it is often transported in improperly packaged and labeled containers.

## Dirty work

Just as the amount of illegally dumped waste is difficult to pin down, so too is hard information on working conditions in maquiladoras. Not only do U.S. and Mexican maquiladora managers deny investigators access to their plants and their workers, but the Mexican government discourages inquiries and health studies. What's more, the U.S. Department of Commerce refuses to share its list of companies participating in the maquiladora program so as not to discourage them from complying with reporting procedures.

High worker turnover rates—6 to 15 percent per month in the states of Chihuahua, Sonora, and Baja California—also make it difficult to survey health effects in maquiladoras. Controlled studies are almost impossible with such an unstable employee population.

What investigators have been able to piece together is that while working conditions in the maquiladoras vary greatly, they are in most cases far inferior to those required in developed countries. Many plants are inadequately ventilated and lighted. Accidents resulting from inattention to safety procedures and the absence of safety equipment are frequent. Nogales maquiladoras reported more than 2,000 accidents in 1989—three times the accident rate of comparable factories on the U.S. side of the border. Sanitation is poor, production quotas are high, noise is often excessive, and machinery is often unsafe.

Workers also receive few rest periods and must perform long hours of microscopic assembly work. And even though many workers regularly handle hazardous materials—especially organic solvents—protective clothing, gloves, and other safeguards routinely required of U.S. industry are rare. To make matters worse, the workers lack safety instruction on the hazardous materials they are using—again a U.S. requirement.

Some plants even allow workers to take home empty contaminated steel drums that once contained hazardous chemicals such as pesticides, solvents, acids, and alkalies. Thousands of these containers are used to store water for domestic purposes throughout the industrial regions of Mexico.

Because of a dearth of studies, the amount of harm caused by such exposure is essentially unknown. But the case of Matamoros, the town where the former U.S. company Mallory Capacitors operated a maquiladora for many years, raises alarming possibilities. The Matamoros School of Special Education has identified 20 retarded children whose mothers were pregnant while employed by Mallory and required to work with PCBs, highly toxic chemicals used in the company's products. PCBs were banned in the United States in 1977 because of their toxicity.

The Matamoros exposures occurred for full workdays over many months. The women often had to reach into deep vats of PCBs with no protection other than rubber gloves. Many of the workers developed the chloracne rash these chemicals typically cause. Recent medical studies in Taiwan and Japan of pregnant women exposed to PCBs reveal the same sort of retardation as in the children of Matamoros. It is very likely that many more children damaged by their mothers' work at Mallory live in other Mexican towns that health researchers have not yet studied. And Matamoros may not be the only town in Mexico where PCBs have caused retardation.

Why does Mexico allow these environmental and occupational abuses to continue? One reason is a lack of resources to combat the problem. SEDUE (Secretariat of Urban Development and Ecology), Mexico's environmental oversight agency, faces financial constraints that limit its ability to regulate the maquiladora industry.

But political constraints play a role as well. The Mexican government enthusiastically supports the maquiladora program. Should SEDUE become too aggressive in its efforts, the government might withdraw the meager environmental funds the agency does receive. Municipal governments also operate from a precarious position. If they complain about hazardous waste dumping or unsafe working conditions—or if they press for taxes to support better sewage treatment facilities, schools, and medical care—the owners might move the plants to other cities or even other countries.

Despite these problems, Mexico has made some progress in environmental regulation. In May 1989, SEDUE required all plants to obtain water discharge permits indicating their compliance with Mexico's rather liberal laws on toxic waste treatment. They may then dump the treated water into the sewer system. Any plant violating this requirement can be fined up to $70,000, and those responsible face a prison sentence of six years. But like most environmental laws in developing countries, this threat is made by an agency that lacks the full backing of its government and the resources to carry out its mission. So far, this effort has produced few results, although a number of companies are now consulting with industrial hygienists and safety engineers to ensure that they will not be fined.

The U.S. government, too, is inching toward cleaning up the border—likewise with few concrete signs of progress. The federal Rio Grande Pollution Correction Act of 1988 aimed at dealing with that river's problems. But its limited scope and lack of financial support led to widespread disappointment and an array of further legislative attempts. Congress considered legislation in 1991 to set up a permanent U.S.-Mexican environmental health commission, in which the EPA and SEDUE would work jointly to evaluate the maquiladoras and explore ways of preventing or punishing environmental abuse along the border.

Unfortunately, none of these proposals addresses the fundamental flaws of the maquiladora program, such as its failure to raise enough taxes to improve infrastructure. Given both governments' acceptance of the present system, no law that would attack the problems at their roots has any serious likelihood of enactment in the near future.

## An international approach

The slowness of the United States in dealing with abuses by the maquiladoras is typical of the way First World nations have responded to the problems caused by the export of hazardous industries. Like the EPA, which devotes only about a tenth of a percent of its budget to its Office of International Affairs, the environmental agencies of other wealthy countries are just beginning to develop concern for the consequences of industry's actions abroad. Nevertheless, it is the exporting nations that need to take the initiative.

The host countries, hungry for jobs and foreign capital, cannot be expected to make the first moves to end unsafe and polluting practices—and they often resent outside pressure to do so. Poorer nations take the position that only after they have attained the standard of living that rich countries enjoy will they adopt the restrictive environmental policies of the First World. What's more, these countries generally lack large, well-funded environmental groups like those in Europe and the United States. Popular support for actions that may impede the growth of the job market and a rise in living standards is virtually nonexistent.

Thus the world's industrialized nations will have to work together to end the shameful practice of exporting obsolete and hazardous technologies and industries. International agreements must replace the perverse incentives that threaten the world's environment.

*While working conditions in the maquiladoras vary greatly, they are in most cases far inferior to those required in developed countries.*

International environmental organizations could help stem many of these problems. The U.N. Environment Programme, for example, has been working with a number of Third World countries to introduce siting requirements for hazardous industries. UNEP is also developing information centers on hazardous materials. The U.N. World Health Organization (WHO) and International Labour Office (ILO) provide some guidance to developing countries on occupational health and safety. But the combined annual budgets of these agencies is only about $3 million, severely hampering their ability to fund environmental research and provide worker education and health inspections. And WHO and ILO have confined their activities mainly to larger employers, while the vast majority of worksites in developing countries are small.

Other global bodies have made laudable attempts to control industry's behavior. The OECD [Organization for Economic Cooperation and Development] Guidelines for Multinational Enterprises, the U.N. Code of Conduct on Transnational Corporations, and the ILO Tripartite Declaration of Principles Concerning Multinational Enterprises and Social Policy attempt to provide a framework of ethical behavior. The ILO declaration of principles, for example, recommends that multinationals inform worker representatives about hazards and protective measures. But stronger medicine is needed.

When industry migrates to developing countries, governments and international lending institutions could require environmental impact assessments. The World Bank, along with other international lenders, now offers to produce such assessments when the host country can't. The bank has also taken steps toward requiring poor countries to put occupational and environmental protections in place as a condition for receiving development capital. Similarly, industrialized countries must insist that companies apply the same safety and environmental regulations to their manufacturing operations abroad as they do at home.

As part of this effort, countries need to cooperate to set global standards for occupational and environmental exposures to dangerous substances. Some newly industrialized countries have formulated lists of chemicals and metals that should receive priority regulation and enforcement. Yet these lists often contain laboratory reagents, rarely used chemicals, and other materials not likely to pose occupational and environmental problems, while omitting many highly toxic substances that see broad use. Industrialized countries therefore need to adopt one set of standards with which all companies manufacturing in poorer countries must comply.

So far, both rich and poor nations see the short-term advantages in the export of hazardous industries but turn a blind eye to long-term harm. In the Third World and the First World alike, the risk of future accidents like Bhopal, the cost of environmental cleanup, and pollution's toll on public health are seldom discussed with candor. But as the developed countries have found, the longer environmental damage and hazardous working conditions continue, the greater the cost of remedying these problems once regulations and enforcement are in place. By disregarding such concerns, First World industries are shifting substantial burdens to those least able to bear them.

# Ceos Are Overpaid

## Graef S. Crystal

*Graef S. Crystal, a former executive compensation consultant, is an ad-junct professor at the Haas School of Business at the University of Cal-ifornia in Berkeley and the author of* In Search of Excess: The Over-compensation of American Executives.

American chief executive officers are overcompensated compared to CEOs in many other countries, such as Japan and Germany. Al-though the average American worker's pay decreased between 1970 and 1990, the average CEO's pay increased to approximately $2.4 million, about 130 times what the average American worker earns. American CEOs often defend their wages by comparing themselves to other high-paid professionals, such as sports stars, movie stars, and investment bankers. This comparison is faulty because, unlike these other professionals, CEOs are not paid ac-cording to their performance; they tend to be paid large salaries and bonuses whether their company does well or poorly.

As the financial boom of the 1980s went bust in a painful recession in 1990 and 1991, the news media turned a spotlight on CEO Disease. Newspapers, magazines, and television news all depicted the modern American CEO as a cross between the ancient Pharaohs and Louis XIV— an imperial personage who almost never sees what the little people do, who is served by boot-licking lackeys, who rules from posh offices, who travels in limousines that have become so long that, like hook and ladder trucks, a second driver will soon have to be hired to steer the back end of the car around tight corners, and in that modern-day equivalent of Cleopatra's barge, the corporate jet, and who is paid so much more than ordinary workers that he hasn't got the slightest clue as to how the rest of the country lives. The oddest thing about all the fuss is that it was right on target.

Ever since money became the medium of exchange, and perhaps even before that, people have debated how much a man's (or, more re-cently, a woman's) labor is worth. Plato told Aristotle that no one in a community should earn more than five times the pay of the lowest-paid worker. Aristotle wrote down what Plato said, but, regrettably, he didn't include the rationale for the statement. During the Middle Ages, Catholic philosophers were caught up in debates over the doctrine of just price, which rested on a belief that there was a divine justification for why one type of labor commanded more pay than another. But whatever pronouncements they made were essentially ignored. At the end of the nineteenth century, J.P. Morgan decreed that chief executives of the Morgan enterprises should not be paid more than twenty times the pay of the lowest worker in the enterprise. (Of course, he may have had a method to his madness, because by keeping a lid on executive pay, he successfully lowered costs and increased profits. And guess who owned all the shares?) Peter Drucker, the management philosopher from Southern California, taking a page from J.P. Morgan, also opined that a CEO should not earn more than twenty times the pay of his lowest worker.

---

*The modern American CEO . . . hasn't got the slightest clue as to how the rest of the country lives.*

---

The notion of some sort of optimum pay ratio has been given concrete expression, from time to time, in government-imposed pay controls. In 1973, President Nixon imposed such controls, not merely on executives but on all workers. The reason? He was alarmed that inflation rate was threatening to push up to as high as 5 percent—a level that today is all but taken for granted. But pay controls, which are merely price controls under a different name (the pay of a person being the price of his labor), have an abundant history of failure. In 1973, for example, the government at first decreed that no executive could receive more than a 5 percent increase in a given year, even if the executive was being promoted and moving to a different company. That notion quickly proved unproductive, since hardly anyone was willing to change employers. Then the government decreed that there would be no pay ceiling when someone was moving to another company; rather, the pay ceiling would be reapplied once the move was made. That revised notion also proved unproductive, since now everyone was willing to change employers, and the executive recruiters had a field day.

Experience with direct price controls has been equally dismal. At one point the government of Iran, out of an apparent desire to help its peasants, decreed that the price of wheat be set lower than the price of grains traditionally fed to animals. The result: the peasantry ate the feed grains themselves and fed the wheat to their animals. The government of the Soviet Union has run aground over the issue of administered prices that distort the use of scarce economic resources.

Frustrated by attempts to control incomes directly, those persuaded that there should be a relatively narrow gap between the pay of top executives and the pay of lowest-paid workers have turned to the tax code. As recently as 1963, an executive who earned taxable income of over $400,000 per year (the equivalent figure today, after correcting for cost of living changes since 1963, would be around $1.7 million) would have been subjected to a marginal tax rate (the rate applicable to any further dollars of taxable income) as high as 91 percent. And President Bush became embroiled with the Democratically controlled Congress over the issue of tax fairness and whether or not the rich were paying too little in the way of taxes.

The fact is that every society, whether that of ancient Rome, the United States, or the Soviet Union, has exhibited extreme ambivalence over the issue of pay differentials between the top and bottom of organizations. Consider the Soviets, for example. Until President Gorbachev blew things apart, that country prided itself as a model of egalitarianism. Prices were controlled, and so were pay levels. A person holding a job equivalent to that of a CEO in America might earn only five times the pay of an ordinary worker. But there was no income tax to reduce that differential further in after-tax terms. And Soviet CEOs received lavish perquisites, including large apartments in Moscow at tiny rents—apartments that ordinary citizens could never aspire to; large dachas in the country; chauffeured Zil limousines; and perhaps most important the privilege of shopping in special department stores. There, the elite could not only buy goods from the West—goods that were totally unavailable to the masses— but they could also buy goods available to the ordinary citizen, *at one-fifth the regular price.* So much for egalitarianism in the Soviet Union.

It is hard to remember what was going on in the United Kingdom before Margaret Thatcher, since she served as prime minister for so long. But there was a time, not too many years ago, when the U.K. used the tax mechanism with a vengeance to assure that after-tax pay differentials were relatively minimal. Taxes rose to 88 percent and beyond. But again reflecting the ambivalence that people feel about compensation, the same British government that was imposing an 88 percent tax rate was permitting its more affluent citizens to deduct their bespoke suits, crafted with loving care in Savile Row, from their tax returns on the basis that they were "uniforms." (U.K. companies today grant fewer perquisites than in the past, but a perennial favorite is the company car. According to *The Economist*, more than half the cars sold in the U.K. each year are bought by companies for their employees.)

---

*The pay of the average worker . . . has dropped around 13 percent, whereas the pay of the average CEO of a major company . . . has risen more than four times.*

---

Perhaps the gamest attempt to control executive pay occurred in Denmark during the late 1960s. There, if an executive's pay rose beyond $53,000 per year, the marginal tax rose to 105 percent. Based on my limited research into Danish taxation, few people in Denmark made more than $53,000 per year in the late 1960s. And those who did, of course, kept far less.

As for the United States, from around the globe comes the message, year after year, that we have the most materialistic society going. We also have an abiding faith in individualism and merit. We have been, and still are, worshipful of the person who comes from humble beginnings and

with great skill rises to the top. Materialism, when combined with individualism and an appreciation of merit, leads to a willingness to offer an
achiever considerable financial rewards. In 1930, when Babe Ruth was the
reigning figure in baseball, a reporter challenged Ruth's very high pay. He
asked Ruth how a mere ballplayer could justify earning $80,000 per
year—$5,000 more than the salary of Herbert Hoover, the president of the
United States. The Babe's reply: "I had a better year than he did!"

*If Fujitsu or NEC are valid comparators for pricing
and labor cost determinations, why are they not
valid comparators for determining the pay of American executives?*

In 1991, the president of the United States, the country's CEO, received a salary of $200,000 per year. We pay some of our entertainers, our
athletes, our investment bankers and lawyers and, especially, our corporation CEOs vastly more than that—every month. (Viewed from a more
global pay perspective, however, the president doesn't make out all that
badly. He has free room and board, and the "room" in this case is a rather
impressive, centrally located mansion, replete with God knows how
many wood-burning fireplaces. And there are many perks, too, including
the use of private helicopters and a private Boeing 747. Among other
things, think about how much it would cost to hire the Marine Band to
play at one of your dinner parties.) But things have gone too far, I believe.
While the pay—in inflation-discounted dollars—of the average American
worker has decreased by almost 13 percent from 1970 to 1980 and by
some 5 percent during the 1980s, the pay of the typical CEO of a major
company—in those same inflation-discounted dollars—has risen more
than three times. (Although the inflation-adjusted pay of the average
worker has declined substantially from 1970 to 1990, that of the average
worker in manufacturing has remained virtually unchanged. It is possible, therefore, that the decrease in real, all-worker pay is illusory and is
largely a function of the shift in jobs from higher-paying manufacturing
industries to lower-paying service industries that has been occurring for
several decades. Nonetheless, a finding that manufacturing pay has been
flat for twenty years, while CEO pay has risen more than three times, is
plenty damning enough.) Where that typical CEO earned total compensation (excluding perquisites and fringe benefits) that was around 35
times the pay of an average manufacturing worker in 1974, a typical CEO
in 1991 earned pay that is around 120 times that of an average manufacturing worker and about 150 times that of the average worker in both
manufacturing and service industries. And U.S. tax policy from 1970 to
1990 has just made matters worse. The total tax load on highly paid executives has declined substantially at the same time that the total tax load
on the average worker has increased—though only by a little. The result
is that, from 1970 to 1990 or so, the pay of the average worker, expressed
in inflation-discounted dollars and adjusted for taxes, has dropped
around 13 percent, whereas the pay of the average CEO of a major company, also expressed in inflation-discounted dollars and adjusted for

taxes, has risen more than four times.

To put things into perspective, a 1991 study I undertook for *Fortune* showed that 86 percent of the CEOs among 200 major companies (the top 100 industrials, the top 50 diversified service companies, and the top 10 from each of the listings for commercial banks, diversified financial institutions, retailers, transportation companies, and utilities) earned $1 million or more per year, while the average CEO earned $1.4 million per year in base salary and annual bonus, and $2.8 million per year when the value of long-term incentives such as stock options was figured in.

And these figures are merely averages. They tell nothing about CEOs whose total compensation is far above the averages—CEOs like J. Peter Grace of W. R. Grace, who in 1973–75 earned about 47 times the pay of an average U.S. manufacturing worker, and in 1987–89 earned about 200 times that worker's pay. Or the late Armand Hammer of Occidental Petroleum, who in the same period went from earning about 41 times the pay of a manufacturing worker to about 138 times. Or Richard Eamer, the CEO of National Medical Enterprises, whose pay ratio rose from about 33 times to about 625 times—a rate of increase that, if applied to the company's nurses, would have guaranteed NME a more than ample supply of professionals in this critically short skill category. And finally, averages say nothing about the person who has most likely earned more compensation than any public-company CEO in history, Steven Ross of Time Warner. His pay rose from about 150 times the pay of an average U.S. manufacturing worker in 1973 to more than 9,000 times the pay of that worker in 1989.

These huge gaps at home between the pay of a CEO and the pay of a worker might be less reprehensible if the same huge gaps could be demonstrated in our major competitors—Japan, Germany, France, and the United Kingdom. But my research reveals that only the U.K. shows signs of catching the U.S. executive compensation virus, and it has only a mild case. In contrast to the 160 times by which the pay of an American CEO exceeds the pay of an average American worker, the corresponding differential in Japan is under 20; and even in the U.K., it is under 35.

---

*The bloated pay packages of American CEOs, with very few exceptions, contain hardly any pay risk.*

---

Throughout this viewpoint, I detail case after case of pay abuse. These cases raise a fundamental question: Is the system rotten around the core, or is it rotten to the core? In other words, are we dealing with a handful of abusers, statistical outliers who, in a perverse way, merely demonstrate that the basic system, the system that applies to thousands of CEOs and other senior executives, is fundamentally sound? Hicks Waldron, formerly the CEO of Avon Products, answered that question in the affirmative when he appeared in May 1991 on the ABC program "Nightline."

Until a couple of years ago, I would have agreed with him. But now I have some grave doubts about the entire system. To be sure, if I remove the key outliers from my 202-CEO, 1991, study for *Fortune*—outliers like Steven Ross and Nicholas Nicholas of Time Warner, Paul Fireman of

Reebok, Anthony O'Reilly of H. J. Heinz, Michael Eisner of Walt Disney, and Rand Araskog of ITT—the average total direct compensation of the group drops from $2.8 million per year to $2.4 million.

Even so, does a pay package of $2.4 million make any sense? Consider first that the CEO receiving $2.4 million per year is earning some 130 times the pay of an average American worker. And as we have seen, that ratio has been widening at an accelerating rate during the last twenty years or so. Consider also that the direction of that pay ratio has been even more steep when the decrease in income tax rates for highly paid executives is taken into account. And most important, consider what our key trading partners—a better word is fierce competitors—are paying their CEOs and other senior executives. There is little comfort in learning that the average pay of an American CEO drops from $2.8 million to $2.4 million after the outliers are removed, when one is forced to consider that the $2.4 million pay figure is still more than seven times higher than a major Japanese company pays its CEO.

---

*There are plenty of sports stars out there who make as much as or more than the average CEO. But no sports star makes as much as the highest-paid CEOs.*

---

In the compensation world, the issue of whether someone is making too much or too little pay is resolved by conducting a survey. That in turn involves selecting a group of comparator companies, measuring how much they pay for a particular position and then comparing the resulting findings to the pay being offered by the company conducting the survey. A key issue here is just who enters the comparator group. Until now, a GM has doubtless included Ford and Chrysler in its comparator group and probably many other major American companies as well. But has a GM thought to include Toyota in its comparator group? Or Nissan? And until now, an IBM has doubtless included AT&T and Apple Computer in its comparator group. But has it thought to include Fujitsu in its comparator group? Or NEC?

It's hard not to believe that GM or IBM study the selling prices of their Japanese competitors when they decide the prices at which to sell their own products. And it's hard not to believe that GM or IBM study how much Japanese companies are paying their factory workers when they analyze their own cost structures. So if Toyota and Nissan, or if Fujitsu or NEC, are valid comparators for pricing and labor cost determinations, why are they not valid comparators for determining the pay of American executives?

When asked that question on a national television talk show, one well-known compensation consultant snorted to the effect that "you can't compare the pay of an American CEO to his Japanese counterpart, because the cultures are so different." Granted the cultures are very different, and, unhappily, so are the products. The Japanese make better cars than we do, and they offer them at better prices. The Japanese culture may be different, but that different culture is killing us. So, to dismiss different executive pay levels in other countries against whom we compete every day in the international and domestic marketplaces is plain fatuous. We had better start including the CEOs of Japanese, German, French, and U.K. companies in our comparator groups, and we had better start doing so right now. If we do, then what do you suppose will happen? Average pay will drop, because that's the result when you add below-average paid executives to a comparator group. And if average pay drops, then American companies with high executive pay scales will no longer be able to say with a clear conscience that "we are simply paying the average and meeting the market." Those same companies are going to have to cut the pay of their CEOs and other senior executives.

If we're paying $2.2 million and the Japanese are paying around $300,000, that gap is going to have to be reduced, if not eliminated entirely. Of course, we can try to persuade the Japanese to pay their executives more. But there's little chance that we'll succeed, because the Japanese are, on the evidence, just too smart to fall into that trap.

Then, too, we need to consider that the bloated pay packages of American CEOs, with very few exceptions, contain hardly any pay risk. Those CEOs get paid hugely in good years and, if not hugely, then merely wonderfully in bad years. So even the defense that high pay is required because of the high risks being taken is shot full of holes.

Is the system rotten around the core or to the core? I'll take Choice B.

## The doctrine of comparable worth

Criticize a highly paid CEO about the size of his pay package and he will be apt to respond along these lines: "You think I'm paid too much? Go look at how much Jose Canseco makes! And Joe Montana. And several hundred other sports stars. Go look at how much Bill Cosby makes. And Jack Nicholson. And several hundred other movie stars, directors, and producers. Go look at how much Felix Rohaytn of Lazard Freres makes working on Wall Street. And corporate adviser Bruce Wasserstein. And several thousand other investment bankers. And while you're at it, don't forget about Michael Milken! Heck, go look at how much Samuel Butler makes at that big New York law firm, Cravath, Swaine & Moore. And Arthur Liman at Paul Weiss. And several thousand other big league attorneys."

Earlier that morning, the very same CEO likely had a bruising conversation with his chief human resources officer concerning the so-called doctrine of comparable worth. That doctrine, which has been heartily embraced by most feminist organizations, holds that there is something wrong with a society that pays a truck driver more than a nurse, an electrician more than a schoolteacher—and so forth. The reason advanced for these disparities is that occupations like nursing and teaching are heavily populated by women, who have long been the victims of pay discrimination. The remedy: Look at positions by comparing their true worth to one another in terms of skills and responsibilities, and then pay them accordingly. A nurse will shortly be discovered to be worth as much as, and most likely more than, a truck driver, and a teacher will be discovered to be worth as much as, or most likely more than, an electrician.

A member of President Reagan's cabinet pronounced the doctrine of comparable worth "loonier than Loony Tunes." CEOs—and the CEOs and top executives of our biggest corporations are almost exclusively male—have routinely railed against it on the basis that it contravenes the one principle that underlies free markets everywhere: the law of supply and demand. Hence, electricians supposedly make more than school-teachers because there are relatively few people who want to be electri-cians and relatively many people who want to be schoolteachers. Upset-ting the law of supply and demand, it is argued, can undermine our entire society. For example, because of union bargaining, New York City's sani-tation workers are paid virtually the same as the city's policemen and fire-men, yet they are highly unlikely to be shot or burned to death in the line of duty. And like New York's policemen and firemen, they get to retire with generous pensions after only twenty years on the job. New York City advertised for a very few sanitation workers; even though picking up the garbage is considered one of society's lowest-ranking occupations, some 3,000 candidates showed up to take the Civil Service examination (which, because of the need to demonstrate realism in such examinations, con-sisted of carrying two garbage cans around an obstacle course in the shortest possible time). Raising the pay of schoolteachers to that of elec-tricians, it is argued, will attract too many candidates to become school-teachers; meanwhile, other occupations will go begging for candidates, and society will end up footing a heavier bill for labor, with the result that inflation and all sorts of other bad things will happen. Obviously, the doctrine of comparable worth is an emotional topic for most CEOs. Rais-ing it is broadly equivalent to zapping them with those electric-shock paddles used in cases of ventricular fibrillation.

Of course, the CEO who was railing about the doctrine of comparable worth in the morning can turn right around in the afternoon and com-pare himself to sports stars, movie stars, investment bankers, and lawyers—all without missing a beat, and all without realizing that he is using the very same comparable worth argument that the social critics have been trying to get him to accept for years.

> There is, arguably, more pay-for-performance built into the remuneration packages of sports stars than there is in the case of CEOs.

Nonetheless, let's look at how much these players in other fields do get paid. First, we have the pay of sports stars as reported in the *Sporting News*, the *New York Times*, and *Forbes*. Roger Clemens of the Boston Red Sox was arguably the highest-paid baseball player in early 1991. He signed a four-year contract worth $21.5 million, or $5.4 million per year. Jose Canseco of the Oakland Athletics probably is the second highest paid; he has a five-year contract worth $23.5 million, or $4.7 million per year. Both Clemens and Canseco, of course, will also earn substantial extra monies for endorsing various commercial products. Indeed, Joe Montana, the star quarterback for the San Francisco Forty-Niners, earned more from product endorsements than he did from being a football player—about $4 million for the endorsements, versus a salary of around $3 million from the Forty-Niners. Even sports stars who have gone over the hill can continue to earn a great deal. *Forbes* estimated the 1991 earnings of Jack Nicklaus, perhaps the greatest golfer who ever lived, at $8.5 million, consisting of a scant $500,000 of prize money and $8 million from product endorsements and appearance fees. When F. Ross Johnson was running RJR Nabisco, Nicklaus was hired to play golf with clients of the company. Nicklaus's pay for a two-year contract: $1 million. However, Nicklaus, good as he is and was, trails another golfer, Arnold Palmer, whose 1991 earnings include $9 million in fees for product endorsements and commercials.

The list can go on and on. Suffice it to say that there are plenty of sports stars out there who make as much as or more than the average CEO. But no sports star makes as much as the highest-paid CEOs. The $200 million or so that accrued to Steve Ross's benefit in 1989, following the acquisition of his company, Warner Communications, by Time Inc., or the $40 million that Michael Eisner of Walt Disney earned in 1988 simply doesn't exist in the sports world.

---

*Perhaps the most important argument undercutting the notion that the pay of CEOs should be compared to that of sports stars concerns the way in which pay is established in the first place.*

---

One also has to consider that there is, arguably, more pay-for-performance built into the remuneration packages of sports stars than there is in the case of CEOs. In his doctoral dissertation (which must have been a lot of fun to research and write), Kenneth Lehn, formerly the Chief Economist of the Securities and Exchange Commission, developed mathematical models to predict the pay of 218 major league pitchers and 358 major league non-pitchers. He could explain more than 70 percent of the variation in pay between these two groups by knowing a number of factors, all of them quite sensible. Several of those factors were directly related to the past performance of the pitchers (their earned run average during the past three seasons, the average number of innings pitched during the past three seasons, and whether or not the pitcher had earned the Cy Young Award), or the non-pitchers (the number of times at bat during the past three seasons, the batting average during the past three seasons, and the number of stolen bases during the past three seasons). Another factor he found to be significant in predicting pay was the number of years the player had been in the major leagues. In the industrial world, people also tend to be paid more for each further year of experience. The only difference is that the limitation on the number of players a team can have dictates that unproductive ballplayers be weeded out quickly; a limitation on the number of purely corporate executives permitted in an industrial company might also prove quite helpful.

Would that the world of industry were as rational as that of major league ballplayers. In my annual surveys for *Fortune,* I can never push the explanation of CEO pay variation beyond about 40 percent. Compare that to the 70 percent pay variation Lehn calculates for baseball players. In short, there is a lot more irrational noise in the way CEOs are paid than there is in the way major league ballplayers are paid.

Kenneth Lehn made another important discovery in his doctoral research. It turns out that most ballplayers' compensation comes only in the form of salary. Product endorsements go to the very few. And the world of complicated annual bonus schemes and exotic long-term incentive plans is alien to the ballpark. The absence of such current incentives means that the pay of a ballplayer tends to be related more to his performance in past seasons than to his performance in this season. To be sure, if the player has a great year or, alternatively, screws up, that result will likely have a significant impact on how much he is paid once his current contract expires and he must negotiate a new one. But that event may be several years away. Because this is so, Lehn found that the more a pay package was predicated on past performance and the greater the length of the pay contract, the likelier it was that the ballplayer would sustain a disability and stay out of commission for a lengthy period. In other words, if you have your pay package "locked," the incentive to come to work each day and to do your best is somewhat blunted, compared to having to put your shoulder to the wheel to receive a current incentive payment.

What Lehn demonstrated here was the opposite proposition to "incentives motivate"; rather, he demonstrated that "lack of incentives demotivates." It's too bad that Lehn's research has not found a wider audience among boards of directors, because if it had, perhaps those boards wouldn't now be so busily engaged in restructuring the pay packages of their company's senior executives to remove any real incentives. As it is, today's typical CEO is given a huge base salary, a guaranteed bonus, a slushy award of free stock that pays off even if the stock price falls by half, a pile of perks, and a lush Golden Parachute just in case he can't find his way to the batter's box. The effect in the industrial world ought to be broadly comparable to that in the ballpark—not so much, perhaps, in a diminished incentive to come to work each day, but rather in the will to play at peak form each day.

> *Whether pay is predicated on past performance or current performance, there is much more pay-for-performance . . . among movie stars than there is among CEOs.*

Perhaps the most important argument undercutting the notion that the pay of CEOs should be compared to that of sports stars concerns the way in which pay is established in the first place. Take Jose Canseco. His agent must have spent a lot of time negotiating with [the late] Walter Haas, the owner of the Oakland Athletics. Haas was no mean slouch when it came to the world of business; among other things, he grew up in the very business-oriented family that has successfully run Levi Strauss for well over a hundred years. One has to presume, therefore, that he would not have agreed to pay Canseco $4.7 million per year unless he thought he could gain something for the Oakland Athletics in the process—increased profit that would flow from the many extra fans who would come to the ballpark to see Canseco play or tune in Athletics' games on television and radio.

Haas's decision to pay Canseco $4.7 million per year resulted from a negotiation remarkably different from the kind CEOs engage in over their own compensation. The paradigm of fair price setting is perhaps the fabled Arabian rug bazaar. The seller begins the negotiations by asking an outlandish price for his merchandise. The buyer responds with a price so low that the seller tears his garments. Much screaming and yelling ensues, punctuated by the buyer's throwing up his hands in disgust and commencing to walk away. Finally, a bargain is struck. The seller is secretly happy, because had he no other recourse, he would have lowered his price even more. The buyer is secretly happy, too, because had he no other recourse, he would have swallowed hard and offered the seller more money. Moreover, when the negotiation between the buyer and seller began, the seller had a pretty good sense of the final prices his competitors were willing to offer. And for his part, the buyer had already been comparison-shopping in the bazaar, as well as learning about the merchandise that was available and its quality. So, all the elements of a good price were present: an informed seller; an informed buyer; and vigorous, indeed, almost violent, arm's-length negotiations.

---

*The pay among law partners is more egalitarian, while the pay among senior executives in major industrial firms is more hierarchical.*

---

Probably the negotiations between Jose Canseco and Walter Haas were a bit less colorful than those in the Arabian rug bazaar. But only a bit less. For his part, Canseco was obviously economically interested in the outcome of the bargaining, and his agent presumably had considerable knowledge useful to the negotiations. In turn, Haas was just as obviously economically interested in the outcome of the bargaining, and he also had considerable knowledge useful to the negotiations. After all, Canseco's agent and Haas have access to pretty much the same information, though each will interpret it differently. Salaries of major league ballplayers are available through the players' union, players' performance statistics are printed in the newspapers every day of the season, attendance figures and TV-radio game ratings are probably available to anyone who knows where to look. A savvy agent presumably finds out how much each 30-second commercial on a local A's or Yankees broadcast brings the club in ad revenue. The club, of course, will claim it's just making ends meet, and the agent will claim the club's rolling in dough. Sounds a lot like the Arabian rug bazaar after all, doesn't it? Finally, the bargaining between a Canseco and a Haas is conducted at arm's length, with each party seeking to maximize his own self-interest. On that basis, therefore, I can only conclude that Jose Canseco is worth the $4.7 million he is being paid. Or at least, he is worth $4.7 million to Walter Haas, the man who has committed to pay the sum. So, if Walter Haas thinks Jose Canseco is worth $4.7 million—especially after a series of arduous negotiations—who, honestly, can say he is not?

How [are] negotiations conducted when the CEO is the seller—in this case, of his own services? Suffice it to say, there's a world of difference. Indeed, several of the elements crucial to setting a valid price are missing altogether: compensation committees of boards of directors tend neither to be shrewd negotiators nor to conduct arm's-length negotiations.

## The entertainment world

Next, we come to pay in the entertainment world as reported in the *New York Times* and *San Francisco Chronicle*. Ever since the time of Louis B. Mayer, Hollywood stars, producers, and, more recently, directors have been earning fortunes. Bill Cosby is reported to have earned $115 million over a two-year period from his various endeavors. Motion picture director Steven Spielberg earned some $87 million, again over two years. And hiring stars like Tom Cruise can cost a studio $8 to $12 million—for a single picture. Jack Nicholson made not a small fortune but a large fortune from playing the Joker in *Batman*. Besides his huge direct pay from the producers, he also received lots of extra remuneration from merchandising the Joker doll and image. Pop stars, too, are lavishly paid. Michael Jackson earned $100 million over the same period. And Madonna raked in $62 million. Indeed, the pay of the key players in the entertainment world makes the pay of sports stars seem like small change.

Like sports stars, the pay of movie stars and pop musicians is predicated heavily on their box-office drawing power, or at least the box-office appeal of the films in which they act, or their recordings. However, a number of enlightened movie studios are cutting deals under which the star takes less fixed compensation and in return receives, if the studio has the upper hand in the negotiations, a percentage of the picture's net profit, or, if the star has the upper hand, a percentage of the gross revenues accruing to the studio. Taking a percentage of gross revenues guarantees, of course, that the star will receive some additional reward for his or her services—even if the film never makes a nickel or loses money. Taking a percentage of the film's profits is a bit more problematic, however, because it exposes the actor to a world that exhibits far more creativity than the actor himself—Hollywood's system of accounting for film profits. Take a blockbuster like *Batman*, for example. It grossed over $250 million. But by the time the Hollywood bean counters got through levying cost after cost against the picture, the film was reported to have lost more than $35 million.

Whether pay is predicated on past performance or current performance, there is much more pay-for-performance, albeit with very high numbers, among movie stars than there is among CEOs. And there is also a pronounced willingness on the part of studio heads to dump a star the moment that he or she is no longer drawing the crowds—or, to put it more succinctly, the moment that he or she is no longer a star.

Once again, however, we have to remember that the pay of these worthies was established after arm's-length bargaining by economically interested parties who have considerable knowledge of what they are doing. True, someone may hire Tom Cruise to make a movie, pay him, say, $12 million, and then watch the movie bomb. Looking backwards, the decision was utterly dumb. But one can look backwards at a stock one bought for $50 and had to sell for $25 and reach the same conclusion. Making a dumb decision on a stock doesn't prove that the price of stocks is set irrationally. After all, no one has yet perfected a way to predict the future.

That a free market, though perhaps one that is crazed, operates in the world of motion pictures can be seen from the huge publicity given to a lengthy memorandum written by Jeffrey Katzenberg, the [former] head of Walt Disney's motion picture units. Katzenberg decried the huge sums being spent on making movies—sums that are for the most part fueled by the high pay of stars. He vowed to fight back and, in a manner reminiscent of Nancy Reagan's anti-drug campaign, to just say no. Perhaps he will not be successful in persuading Hollywood's superstars to cut their pay, but his counterpressure is what free markets are all about.

## Investment bankers and lawyers

There is also the princely paid world of investment bankers. According to a front-page article in the *Wall Street Journal*, Bruce Wasserstein's company, Wasserstein Perella & Co., one of the hottest investment banking firms of the 1980s, received a $5.5 million fee from a single client, Interco, for "five months of work by perhaps two dozen people, most of them working on Interco only part-time." And the pay of partners of Goldman, Sachs, perhaps Wall Street's most prestigious investment banking firm, is rumored to be in the many millions per partner in a good year. And Michael Milken, the Beverly Hills investment banker who earned more than $500 million in pay in a single year and who was the driving force behind the now-discredited junk market, earned about 40 cents per hour under what you might think of as a pay contract with a term of up to ten years that he negotiated with the federal government.

The same two arguments crop up again. First, there is a fair amount of pay-for-performance among investment bankers. If you set up and then tout a deal that turns out to be a disaster, there's a good chance that other companies will turn elsewhere for investment advice. There's a certainty that the client you hurt will turn elsewhere. Second, though Wall Street pros are rumored to be brilliant, they still have to negotiate their fees with some pretty smart people on the other side—people like the chief financial officers of major corporations. And in these days when so-called relationship banking (in which a company sticks with its investment banking firm year in, year out, rather than letting various investment banking firms compete for each deal) has fallen on hard times, pay-for-performance is stronger than ever.

There is also a third aspect to consider. If Wasserstein Perrella or Goldman, Sachs loses money, then Bruce Wasserstein and the partners of Goldman, Sachs will also lose money. Not so with most CEOs. They can make huge amounts of money, but it is hard for them to lose much money. (Outright losses can be generated to the extent the CEO has substantial shareholdings in his company, but most CEOs do not.) No matter how many times I have touted them, negative bonuses—the kind where the CEO writes a check to the company—have just never caught on.

And there is even a fourth aspect to consider. Working on Wall Street is an exceedingly volatile experience. During the 1980s, it seemed that anyone with a big-school MBA could trot down to Wall Street and rake in a million a year before he or she reached the age of thirty. The pay of Wall Streeters had anti-gravity characteristics—high every year, no matter what. All that has changed since the stock market crash of 1987. Thousands upon thousands of jobs in the investment banking world have been lost, and more than a few highly paid investment bankers are currently said to be considering driving taxicabs.

Finally, we come to the lawyers. According to *The American Lawyer*, the sixty-six partners of Cravath, Swaine & Moore earned $1.5 million per partner in 1990. Even at the tenth-most profitable law firm—Fried, Frank, Harris, Shriver & Jacobson—the average pay for each of that firm's 107 partners was $835,000.

Now pay of $1.5 million per year can't hold a candle to the pay of your typical big company CEO. But what is impressive about the pay in law firms is the *sheer number* of people who can earn relatively large sums of money. Or, to put it another way, the pay among law partners is more egalitarian, while the pay among senior executives in major industrial firms is more hierarchical. Even among the highest-paying industrial firms, it would be difficult to find the top sixty-six executives earning an average of $1.5 million per year.

To echo the famous line in *Casablanca*, the usual suspects must be rounded up once again. First, one has to suppose that pay-for-performance exists among law firms. If you're looking for a good attorney, you are highly unlikely to retain one who has a terrible win/loss ratio or one who routinely gets you into hot water with the SEC [Securities and Exchange Commission] or the IRS. So it is no accident that the most highly regarded law firm in the United States, Cravath, Swaine & Moore, also produces the most profits for each of its partners. Second, though there may be less arm's-length bargaining over fees between a company and its law firm than there is in the world of sports, movies, and investment banking (mainly because of the imperfect knowledge that the buyers of legal services have about how much work is required to accomplish a given task, and also because of the lack of ability to forecast the direction in which the give-and-take of legal battling will head), a law firm that charges way too much for its services will likely get its comeuppance eventually. Already, a movement is afoot among major companies to seek alternative dispute resolutions (mediation, arbitration, mini-trials, and so forth) as a way of reducing the growing cost of litigation. Finally, lawyers, like investment bankers, can lose real money if their firm sustains a loss in a given year. A well-known, and huge, law firm—Finley, Kumble—self-destructed. One has to suppose that its partners took substantial hits to their personal balance sheets, given that law firms use a partnership form of organization that leaves partners exposed to losses sustained by the partnership.

In summary, there are quite a few people in other fields who are making nearly as much as and sometimes a lot more than your typical big company CEO. But there are lots of good reasons why this is so. And because those reasons don't figure very heavily in the compensation of CEOs, the argument that a CEO should earn what he earns—or even earn more—because of what sports stars or movie stars or investment bankers or top lawyers earn simply doesn't hold much water.

# Corporate Social Responsibility Harms Business

Douglas J. Den Uyl

*Douglas J. Den Uyl is a professor of philosophy at Bellarmine College in Louisville, Kentucky.*

Business is morally good because it combines what one should do (duty) with what one wants to do (interest). It is a CEO's duty to maximize profits for the firm's owners, and because the CEO's personal financial success is dependent on that of the company, it is in his interest to do so. Corporate social responsibility diminishes profits and undermines the harmony between duty and interest in at least five ways. While wealth is not the only or the highest good in life, it must be the central good in business.

It is often argued that we are in desperate need of courses or training in business ethics because business is an area more devoid of ethics than other endeavors. Indeed, it is usually assumed that there is something *fundamentally* at odds between business and ethics. Business must be tamed by ethics because by itself business has no natural affinity with ethics—it may even be antithetical to ethics! Our point in this viewpoint, however, is exactly the opposite. Business and ethics are allied with each other at the fundamental level and only conflict at the fringes.

Aristotle held that the morally perfect individual was one in whom knowledge of what one *ought* to do was fully integrated with what one *desired* to do. If one knew what the good was and desired something else, that was a sign of moral imperfection. By the same token, if one simply did what one wanted without giving any thought to what was good, that too was a sign of imperfection. The morally good person, we might say then, thoroughly blends his or her desires with what is morally good. This could be described as the coincidence of duty and interest.

The sorts of philosophers that have dominated our own age by contrast have seen the interested and the moral to be either in inherent or

Douglas J. Den Uyl, "Duty and Interest," *Freeman*, July 1994. Reprinted courtesy of the Foundation for Economic Education.

67

likely conflict. Immanuel Kant, for example, tells us that the presence of interest lessens or destroys the moral quality of an act. J.S. Mill worries about the narrowness of self-interest preventing one from acting for the good of the whole. And even Adam Smith has qualms about the connection between self-interest and social well-being.

All these more abstract worries about morality and desire would certainly have an impact upon Business Ethics. For if the two really are in necessary conflict, it looks as though business—which is apparently grounded in interested pursuits—will be hard pressed to incorporate anything like ethical duty.

There is the possibility nonetheless that the very essence of business may just consist in this Aristotelian ideal! For that to be the case, duty and interest must not only be harmonized such that what is in one's interest also turns out to be one's duty, but also that in being subject to a certain obligation one is thereby furthering one's interest. While other professions, e.g., law and medicine, may suggest (undoubtedly somewhat naively) that the interests of others (the patient or client) take precedence over one's own, business turns out to be essentially rooted in the proposition that our own interests and the interests of others are co-extensive.

## The convergence of duty and interest

The rudiments of our point are found in the simple act of trade or free exchange. With respect to the interest side of the issue exchanges are presumably in the interests of all parties or they would not take place. The act of trade seems to leave out, however, the notion ordinarily associated with "duty," namely of there being some sort of moral obligation to others. If it were the case, however, that one made exchanges that were not only in one's interest but which one had an obligation to others to make, then duty and interest would be harmonized. As strange as it may at first seem, the modern corporate manager is in the position of having both the duty and interest to engage in trade.[1]

As a fiduciary of the corporation a manager has a duty or obligation to act in the interests of that corporation. Although it may seem as though there is now the same old possibility for conflict between one's interest and one's duty if what would be good for the corporation would not be so good for oneself, this perception is largely illusory in business. Indeed, if managers come to see their personal business interests as being in conflict with the business of the corporation, then we would describe the corporation as badly managed. To insure against this sort of conflict, corporations offer equity and other incentives to tie one's wealth to that of the corporation. In a business environment it would actually be strange to think of the corporation's interest as taking precedence over that of the individual (or vice versa). As a business enterprise, the assumption is that everyone involved is interested in personal wealth maximization and corporate life (as opposed to, say, self-employment) is the mode chosen to that end. Consequently, there is no prior or essential split between self and corporate interests or obligations.

Perhaps one is inclined to object that numerous cases of conflicts of interest between managers and corporations can and do occur. A manager may wish, for example, to give some relative the contract for supplies rather than the firm with the highest quality at the lowest price. Or perhaps one is thinking of the conflicts that are sometimes said to exist between managers and stockholders (owners) over such matters as the sale of the business in a "hostile" takeover. It is not our claim here that such conflicts cannot or do not take place. Rather, our claim is that the legal conception of a "fiduciary," while perfectly appropriate to business law, can mislead one when it comes to understanding the essential character of business.

In law, a situation is corrected or operating normally when the fiduciary fulfills his or her obligation, whatever the personal interests involved. In business, by contrast, a situation is normal only when one's interest is engaged. If one is simply doing one's duty, a potential (if not actual) management problem exists. The sorts of conflicts that may arise in the business world are not solved, in other words, by the appropriate fulfillment of a role. They can only be solved when the appropriate actions are motivated by personal commitment. In business one does not make commitments to obligations, but rather one's obligations grow out of one's commitments. A business, therefore, has the appropriate managers when those managers see their own best opportunity for maximizing their wealth as being co-extensive with the work they are doing.

## Disrupting the harmony

Now there are many factors that serve to undermine this happy coincidence of duty and interest in the modern world. Some of these, we must admit, may be generated from the quasi-bureaucratic nature of the large modern multinational corporation. Yet the most significant of these factors arise from the present political climate and the social/moral claims used to support it. In business ethics the issue is put most clearly in the debate over corporate social responsibility.

The controversy centers around Milton Friedman's claim that corporations have no social responsibility beyond wealth maximization within the "rules of the game."[2] This is thought to be too limited and too economically centered a view for most writers in the field, and thus they would speak of a more expanded sense of social responsibility for business.[3] Businesses are being asked to consider the good of society as a whole, or certain aspects of society (sometimes called these days "stakeholders"), as being of equal or greater consideration than "the bottom line." Yet what can be said for Friedman's position is that it, rather than the alternatives, best serves the harmony of duty and interest as we have described it here.

Friedman's argument is quite simple: it would violate one's contractual obligations to the owners (stockholders) if one pursued anything other than wealth maximization, for that is precisely what managers were *hired* to pursue. So as managers seek profits for the firm, they are both satisfying an obligation to others as they achieve what is to their own benefit. Moreover, they are doing so in a *community* of wealth pursuers (i.e., among others doing likewise).[4] It must be the case then that to oppose Friedman's position is to claim that we ignore or otherwise diminish the pursuit of profits for the sake of other "responsibilities." In doing that, however, the harmony between duty and interest that is established within the community of wealth pursuers would be undermined in at least five ways:

1. By overriding the contractual relationship in favor of vague, limitless, and all-encompassing "obligations," there is no certainty that one has satisfied one's obligations in a business context and thus little chance of harmonizing one's interest with them.

2. With the contractual model, one's obligations flow from one's commitments; but in the corporate social responsibility model, one's commitments are to be defined by one's obligations implying, as we noted above, the diminishment of interest.

3. The idea of a social responsibility beyond that of wealth maximization necessarily subordinates the latter to the former and thus, at least temporarily, drives a wedge between what the individual is in fact pursuing and what he or she ought to be pursuing.

4. Indeed, the additional "obligations" suggest the moral inferiority of the pursuit of wealth, so that if one takes a greater interest personally in the pursuit of wealth within a business context one is necessarily at odds with what one is supposed to be interested in morally.

5. Corporate social responsibility undermines the individualism implied by the harmony of duty and interest by conceiving of the corporation as the locus of moral responsibility rather than the individuals who jointly compose it.

---

*Business turns out to be essentially rooted in the proposition that our own interests and the interests of others are co-extensive.*

---

These reasons, and undoubtedly others, should indicate how current conceptions of corporate social responsibility undermine not only the ideal harmony we have been discussing, but also the very ethos of business itself. For we can now realize that what constitutes a *business* context or relationship is one where the production or pursuit of wealth is central both morally and operationally. Corporate social responsibility decentralizes the role of wealth in business in favor of other ends, and in this respect undermines the very ethos of business.

One might say in response to all this, "Who cares about the harmony anyway? Isn't it the case that morality essentially is a conflict between what one wants to do and what one ought to do. And moreover, don't such things as pollution, poverty, unemployment, and illiteracy take precedence over wealth and the greed that comes with its pursuit?" These are complex questions with arguable underlying assumptions. They cannot be fully answered here. But if one is open to the idea that harmonizing duty and interest might be a good thing, then perhaps one might be willing to consider approaches to social problems that are more in accord with maintaining that harmony. Much has been written about various market-oriented approaches to all these issues—approaches that provide an alternative social vision to the politically dominated one espoused by advocates of corporate social responsibility. To admit that poverty and pollution are problems is to say absolutely nothing about the appropriate way to address them.

What is more pertinent to our point is the basic question of why we should care whether there is any coincidence between duty and interest in the first place. As we have noted, business does in fact approximate the ideal. But why should one care about the ideal itself? The reason is that it is within this harmony of duty and interest that one finds the basis for the moral legitimacy of business itself. It is not because of the benefits provided us that business is morally justified, nor is it because business "behaves" itself in appropriate ways. Business is at root morally legitimate because the good it seeks (wealth) is appropriate for human existence and can be sought without any fundamental conflict between what is good for oneself and what is appropriate conduct towards others. To insure that both are in harmony requires that we do nothing to threaten the centrality of wealth which makes that harmony possible.

Is wealth then the highest or only good? Is its pursuit constrained by nothing? Wealth is neither the only nor highest good in human life. It is and must be, however, the central good in *business*. That means that when it comes to business, other ends must be considered in light of wealth, even if another end takes priority in other contexts. It also means that the social conditions for the integration of various ends and the pursuit of any end must be respected. This is another way of saying that basic individual rights must be respected.[5] But since that sort of respect is an obligation one has in all contexts under all circumstances, we have no *additional* obligation but rather one that makes all other social obligations meaningful. We can only begin to know what obligations we have towards others when we know what their rights are. In addition, we can only begin to cooperate effectively with others when we do so on the basis of mutual interest. And if our interests can become our obligations we shall more likely understand the moral value and propriety of business than if we think in terms of trying to transform obligations into interests or of making obligations independent of interests altogether.

## Notes

1. We focus mainly on the corporation and its managers, since this is the main focus of most of the writing on business ethics.

2. This position is reprinted in most business ethics texts. For example, see W. Michael Hoffman and Jennifer Mills Moore (eds.) *Business Ethics* (New York: McGraw-Hill, 1975), pp. 153–157.

3. One need only consult the essays conjoined with the one mentioned in the last note to confirm this point. Any other business ethics text would serve as well.

4. This argument does not rule out the possibility that some things which at first seem like they might detract from profitability might in the end contribute to it and are therefore legitimate.

5. I have expanded on these points more fully in "Corporate Social Responsibility," *Business Ethics and Common Sense*, Robert W. McGee (ed.) (Westport, Conn.: Quorum Books, 1992), pp. 137–151.

# Corporations Are Responsible Only to Their Owners

## Doug Bandow

*Doug Bandow is a senior fellow at the Cato Institute, a libertarian public policy research foundation. He is the author of* The Politics of Plunder: Misgovernment in Washington.

Corporations are formed to make a profit by providing the goods and services people need and want. They should not be forced to give donations to charities, provide benefits for their employees, or underwrite the local symphony, although they should be free to do so if they choose. The best way for a corporation to serve society is to satisfy its customers' needs and wants in an efficient manner.

Many commentators and lawmakers increasingly seem to believe that business owes everything to everyone.

There was a time when even the contention that businesses should contribute to local charities was viewed as controversial. Milton Friedman, for instance, long championed the position that such outlays, however well-intended, were essentially the theft of shareholder assets. In his view, the corporation was responsible to the shareholders and no one else. (Firms were, of course, bound to respect the rights of others, which warranted barring them from dumping wastes in other people's yards, for example.)

For years the Friedman position seemed to be widely accepted, even though it was often honored only in the breach. Since the New Deal, for instance, the federal government has set maximum working hours and minimum wages for many employees, an action presumably based on some judgment as to business's "social responsibility" to its employees. Nevertheless, few people saw this "responsibility" as being particularly far-reaching. Indeed, the law once prohibited companies from making charitable donations; only in 1953 did a landmark lawsuit clear the way

Doug Bandow, "What Business Owes to Cure Society's Woes," *Business and Society Review*, Spring 1992. Reprinted with permission.

for firms to support higher education.

But over the last three decades social responsibility has become part of the political lexicon and even many businessmen support the concept. In 1981, for instance, President Ronald Reagan created the Task Force on Private Sector Initiatives. The group, made up of representatives of business, government, and philanthropic enterprises, took an expansive view of corporate responsibility. For instance, task force member Kenneth Dayton argued that "the business of business is serving society, not just making money." Task force staff member E.B. Knauft, who was a social responsibility officer at Aetna Life & Casualty, tried to make this position more acceptable to business by contending that social responsibility and community partnerships (to decide on the use of donations) were "in the company's self-interest."

---

*A firm is solely responsible to its owners.*

---

And the so-called independent sector, which depends on corporate funds, has not been shy about telling firms that they have an obligation to contribute. Said James A. Joseph, president of the Council on Foundations: "The corporate charter is a social as well as a legal contract, which makes each corporation a trustee of the public good. . . . Maximizing profits is not by itself a socially desirable end."

Not only are firms to give, but they are to allow others to decide on how the money is used. The Reagan task force, for instance, advanced the idea that "community partnerships" should direct the distribution of philanthropic resources. In effect, corporate largesse was to be treated as belonging to the community and its disposition was to be directed by public-spirited officials, presumably such as Joseph, who once complained that those providing aid directed at minorities were establishing "the priorities of the black community."

While the task force's expectation that firms should not only give but also yield control over their funds may seem somewhat arrogant, at least it only applied to funds freely given. More serious are legislators who apparently share this attitude as they vote to increasingly regulate business. For instance, many states now require firms to offer health insurance and family leave; similar measures have been proposed in Congress. Companies must maintain health insurance for laid-off workers, adopt affirmative action programs (often through informal quotas) for minorities and women, and reconfigure their buildings and take other steps to accommodate the disabled. Firms must provide public notification before they close plants; some localities have attempted to seize firms to prevent them from closing; other municipalities have attempted to take over local sports franchises. Business is a popular target for tax increases for all sorts of purposes.

## Duty or duress?

Unfortunately, the almost continuous expansion of the belief in business's social responsibility is the result not of reasoned debate but of the corrupting influence of political power. Most of these regulations have developed as influential interest groups decided that business should do something and lobbied the government to make their preferences law. The justification offered to the public was that this was business's responsibility. But just what do companies owe? And to whom? The minimalist position is probably held by Nobel laureate Friedman and Irving Kristol, among others. In their view, a firm is solely responsible to its owners—the shareholders in the case of a corporation. Thus, for managers to engage in other endeavors, such as charitable giving, is to violate their fiduciary duty.

Although these views are dismissed as quaint by today's apostles of corporate social responsibility, Friedman and Kristol have gotten the large picture correct. Corporations are specialized institutions created for a specific purpose. They are only one form of enterprise in a very diverse society with lots of different organizations. Churches exist to help people fulfill their responsibilities toward God in community with one another. Governments are instituted most basically to prevent people from violating the rights of others. Philanthropic institutions are intended to do good works. Community associations are to promote one or another shared goal. And businesses are established to make a profit by meeting people's needs and wants.

Should not business nevertheless "serve" society? Yes, but the way it best does so is by satisfying people's desires in an efficient manner. There are, in fact, few tasks more pressing than to provide what Nobel laureate Friedrich A. von Hayek calls "the social product which is now maintaining a human population of this world 400 or 500 times as large as that which man could achieve in the natural hunting and gathering stage." And this productivity, in his view, "is owed only to the division of labor, skills, and knowledge." This division of labor applies not only to individuals but also to institutions.

In short, businessmen should concentrate on being good businessmen. They shouldn't be charged with saving men's souls. Nor should they be expected to house the homeless, preserve the community, or do any of many other important tasks for which other institutions have been created.

Does this mean that firms have no responsibilities other than making money? Of course not, just as individuals have obligations other than making money. But while firms have a duty to respect the rights of others, they are under no obligation to promote the interests of others. The distinction is important. Companies have responsibilities not to spew harmful pollutants into people's lungs and break contracts with their workers. They do not, however, have any obligation to underwrite a local symphony or provide their workers with popular benefits, such as family leave.

## Fighting back

This does not mean that firms should be prohibited from promoting other goals when they desire to do so. In this regard, at least, Friedman and Kristol are wrong about the issue of corporate philanthropy. E.B. Knauft may be right when he argues that charitable giving promotes a firm's bottom line. Such "selfishness" is a perfectly honorable reason for giving—after all, everyone benefits. Similarly, offering family leave or improved health care benefits may be a savvy step to attract top-quality workers. Going beyond the norm in emphasizing a commitment to pollution control may help attract environmentally conscious consumers.

Even if the firm receives no direct financial benefit from such activities, they are legitimate as long as the stockholders are aware of management's activities. When Levi Strauss went public, for instance, it informed prospective shareholders that it intended to continue its active program of charitable giving. If shareholders are willing to effectively funnel some of their resources through one or more firms to promote philanthropy, family bonding with a newborn, or whatever, then so be it. But this is different from philanthropic organizations browbeating firms to give or government mandating that they do so.

Social responsibility has become a catchword on the left, an excuse for ever-expanding government control of business. It's time that business fought back and explained that it has no more special responsibilities than anyone else. In the end, society will benefit most if business concentrates on doing its job well, rather than trying to solve the rest of the world's problems.

# 9
# Corporate Philanthropy Is Counterproductive

Jeffrey H. Coors

*Jeffrey H. Coors is president of ACX Technologies, an industrial products manufacturing business that is a former subsidiary of Adolph Coors Company, and a trustee for Hillsdale College in Michigan.*

People were created to give of themselves for the betterment of others, and Americans have taken this belief to heart by being the most giving nation in the world. American corporations also donate a substantial portion of their profits to charities. However, corporate giving is often motivated by companies' self-interest, and it is an ineffective way to address the nation's social and economic problems. Corporations should give back to the community not by donating to charities but by distributing their dividends to the owners, who can then decide individually which charities they want to support.

Throughout history, most of the world has thought of giving and self-sacrifice as a means of earning something in return. But the Judeo-Christian tradition views giving and self-sacrifice as a voluntary reflection of God's benevolent nature in whose image we were created. Giving of ourselves and our resources is being what we were created to be.

Millions of Americans believe this to be true. We are the most giving nation on earth. There is no tradition of benevolence that can compare in Asia, Latin America, Africa, or even Europe. Nowhere in the world is there a United Way or a Cancer Society like ours. No other nation supports missionaries to the same extent, and none can compare with America in support for private, independent education. In many countries, congregations do not even pass the offering plate. Mandatory church taxes pay for everything, from the priest, the organist, the choir, and the ushers to the heat, water, and electricity. They are the most lifeless churches you have ever entered.

When everything is taken care of by government, the spirit of voluntary commitment is lost. In contrast, it is our Judeo-Christian heritage

Jeffrey H. Coors, "The Meaning of Corporate Stewardship," *Imprimis*, June 1993. Reprinted courtesy of *Imprimus*, Hillsdale College.

that has inspired our giving. Americans donate about $100 billion to
charity each year, mostly in the form of individual contributions. Re-
markably, poor Americans give a higher percentage of their incomes than
do their more affluent neighbors. Corporate America currently gives $5
billion, or five percent, of all charitable giving each year. This is a relatively new source of philanthropy, begun during World War I, when corporations were urged to declare "Red Cross Dividends." These were paid
with after-tax dollars; they were not considered legitimate business expenses by the IRS. Nonetheless, many businesses went along. During the
Depression, other charities like Community Chest and United Way
adopted the idea. But not until 1936 did the IRS declare that a charitable
contribution could be a deductible business expense, and even then it
had to directly benefit the business. This ruling actually allowed management to circumvent shareholders in making the decision to contribute.
Then in 1953 a gift to Princeton University triggered a court battle that
led the IRS to allow gifts to any organization without regard to the best
interests of the business. The only limit, which is still in effect today, stip-
ulated that gifts must be no more than five percent of a corporation's pretax earnings. Very few corporations give the maximum.

*The profits belong to all who invest in expectation
of earning a return, so shouldn't the profits of a
corporation be reserved for the benefit of the owners?*

There are plenty of people who will tell you that five percent is not
enough. But we ought not ask whether the corporate community "does
its fair share." We ought, rather, to ask: "What is corporate responsibility?" This is a question that goes to the nature of business itself. Very simply, a business sells goods and/or services to people who want them. By
law, a business corporation is authorized to act in place of a person, even
though it may be owned by many. The profits belong to all who invest in
expectation of earning a return, so shouldn't the profits of a corporation
be reserved for the benefit of the owners?

Of course, the owners have a duty and obligation to consider how
they will dispose of their profits. The matter is simple in a proprietorship
or partnership with a small number of owners: The parties may meet and
choose to give to worthy causes. It gets more complicated in the case of a
so-called public company, which may have thousands of shareholders.
How can all be consulted on disposition of the profits? I think the solution is very simple: pay out the profits as dividends and let the owners decide what to do with the money.

But in recent years corporations have learned from politicians to become very skilled at giving away other people's money while making
themselves feel good about it. Many arguments are raised to justify corporate giving. One of them is genuine altruism. People are moved by pure
motives to contribute, and that is commendable. A second argument is
that the needs are so great that they require corporate rather than individual resources. A third justification is that giving creates goodwill in the
community. This view is based on the idea that it is important for corpo-

rations to be good citizens and to contribute to the community. (It sounds appealing until one realizes that it is possible to give back to the community simply by lowering prices.)

The current buzzword in corporate giving is "enlightened self-interest." If you make the world a better place, people will buy more of what you have to sell. Enlightened self-interest also creates good public relations. Whole textbooks have been written on this kind of "cause-related marketing." Huge P.R. departments create photo opportunities for corporate heads to shake hands with the leaders of local charities and to hand them checks. The results of this kind of philanthropy are measured by the good it does for the company, not the good it does for the recipient.

There is also a great deal of peer pressure to conform in the corporate world. If a worthy cause is in need and most of the community is giving to that organization, a company becomes conspicuous by its absence. And corporate philanthropy can help avoid trouble. Dozens of special interest groups routinely target corporations and issue the threat of a boycott in order to secure contributions. Often these contributions are in reality just like "protection money" businesses are forced to pay to the underworld.

Corporate philanthropy has also funded hundreds of legitimate causes meant to solve our nation's problems. But the poor seem to get poorer, the plight of the inner city has grown, and many citizens have become more and more dependent upon the federal government. Corporate philanthropy has helped foster that dependence. In the Capital Research Center's *Patterns of Corporate Philanthropy* the philanthropic contributions of the top 250 corporations in the country are graded. Gifts to a conservative organization merit an "A." Contributions to a non-ideological group are awarded a "C," while benefactions to leftist/liberal causes earn a "D" or an "F." The scores for each company are then averaged. Since the book was first published in 1986, there has not been a single top corporation with a record of giving that deserved an "A" rating. Only 13 percent in the last study had a "B"; 24 percent had a "C"; 52 percent had a "D"; 11 percent had an "F." I question the motives and values of companies that give shareholder profits to organizations that encourage further dependency on government. Is this "enlightened self-interest"?

---

*Many citizens have become more and more dependent upon the federal government. Corporate philanthropy has helped foster that dependence.*

---

It is also clear that corporate philanthropy has been a poor substitute for personal philanthropy. It has not only been widely perverted by businesses and special interest groups, but it has not been very effective in addressing the problems it seeks to solve. In this context, it is more important than ever that we develop guidelines for personal philanthropy.

Here are the guidelines I would suggest:

(1) Giving is an individual opportunity to reflect the benevolent nature of a loving God. Give so that you might become the person you were created to be.

(2) Support people and causes with which you are personally involved. Give more than just money to those you are helping; stand with them and help them personally.

(3) The Bible says that the measure you use to give, whether large or small, will be used to measure what is given back to you. It is important to consider the biblical tithe as an appropriate standard. It does not have to be 10 percent, but it should be a specific amount you set aside as soon as you receive your paycheck.

(4) Do not wait until you are established in the world; you will never be established in the world. You will never reach a point at which you have "arrived" and can begin giving.

(5) Give privately, not seeking recognition for your work; it is for others' benefit, not your own, that you are giving.

(6) Be a cheerful giver. The joy of helping others far exceeds the joy of helping yourself.

# 10

# Multinational Businesses Can Be Socially Responsible

## Robert D. Haas

*Robert D. Haas is chairman of the board and chief executive officer of Levi Strauss & Co.*

Ethical misconduct by multinational corporations erodes the public's confidence in business. When operating overseas, corporations should ensure that products are being made in a manner that protects the company's reputation and is consistent with the company's values. By establishing and enforcing guidelines for ethical conduct, both at home and overseas, businesses can protect their investments and reputations.

> Editor's Note: The following speech was delivered before The Conference Board, a business research organization, on May 4, 1994, as part of a two-day conference on business ethics.

We are meeting at a time when it seems that in every facet of contemporary life, people are placing self-interest ahead of ethical values. Pick up almost any day's edition of the *New York Times* and accounts of faltering ethical standards are chronicled in virtually every section of the paper. For purposes of my comments today, however, I want to focus on the business pages, since business and ethics is what we're here to talk about.

It wasn't so long ago that everyone had proclaimed that the "greed is good" spirit of the 1980s was dead and that the 1990s represented a return to basic values. But an honest evaluation of current business conduct contradicts that assessment; for example:

• Executives of American Honda are criminally indicted by Federal prosecutors for accepting bribes from dealers in exchange for franchises and hot-selling cars. Thirteen executives face potential prison terms that total 165 years behind bars.

• Corruption and mismanagement cause Gitano Jeans to lose its largest retail customer. The company's fortunes collapse. It's forced to file for bankruptcy and is ultimately sold.

Robert D. Haas, "Ethics—a Global Business Challenge," *Vital Speeches of the Day*, June 1, 1994. Reprinted with permission.

• Prudential Securities is sued by its investors who allege it inappropriately sold limited partnerships. The scandal costs hundreds of millions of dollars, and the inquiry into possible corporate misdeeds extends into the company's most senior ranks.

• National Medical Enterprises agrees to pay more than $300 million to settle charges of health insurance fraud and patient abuse.

It should hardly come as a surprise that such incidents have led to an erosion of public confidence and an eruption of distrust in the major institutions of our society—including business.

But these accounts of ethical misconduct are not unique to the U.S.— as recent scandals in Great Britain, Japan, Brazil, Russia and elsewhere suggest. In my comments today, however, I intend to talk primarily about what's going on here in America.

While price fixing conspiracies, bribery, fraud and business collusion are not the norm of contemporary business practice, they occur far more frequently than we care to acknowledge—and clearly more often than is permissable to gain the level of public trust and support that business requires to thrive.

What is most puzzling about instances of business wrongdoing is that they clearly contradict both the values that are held by most of us as individuals and the collective standards we have established for appropriate business behavior.

When pressed about his company's payment of bribes to Italian political parties in the '80s, the chairman of Olivetti made the startling confession that he personally authorized the payment of bribes and added that he would do it again to protect his company's interests.

In his famous essay on civil disobedience, Henry David Thoreau wrote that a corporation "has no conscience, but a corporation of conscientious men is a corporation with a conscience." I'd like to think that if Thoreau were writing today he would have spoken of both men *and women* with a conscience, though regrettably the corporate world remains more of a male enclave than it should be.

---

*Doing the right thing from Day One helps avoid future setbacks and regrets.*

---

If Thoreau is correct, and I believe he is, how do we help honorable men and women confront and address the ethical challenges they face in the everyday world of work? This is the puzzle all of us must work to solve.

In my remarks this morning, I'd like to talk about some of the ethical struggles that we've faced at my own company [Levi Strauss & Co.] and how we've dealt with them.

I'd like to begin by conducting a brief quiz. By the way, these are the same questions I raise with my associates at Levi Strauss & Co. when I lead one of our ethics training programs.

As I ask these five questions, please respond by raising your hands.

First, how many of you consider yourselves to be ethical people?

How many of you believe that it's important for business to function in an ethical manner?

How many of you believe that you know an ethical dilemma when you see it?

How many of you feel there are clear answers to ethical problems?

Now, how many of you believe that I always know an ethical dilemma when it arises and always know how to resolve it?

Clearly, all of us feel strongly about ethics in the abstract. But at the same time, each of us is keenly aware of the struggle we face as ethical dilemmas arise. It is this common struggle—between our own desire to be ethical and the competing pressures of business performance—that brings us here today.

I should admit that when I approached the microphone this morning, I did so with some trepidation because of this very fact. While I am honored to be able to keynote this important, two-day conference, like everyone in this room, we at Levi Strauss & Co. struggle every day with how to create a business culture that promotes ethical behavior.

All of us can cite our own experiences about ethical problems we've encountered or witnessed firsthand. The real value of this conference is that each of us can offer our own ideas about how to help managers and employees apply their own high ethical standards in the workplace, so that they don't have to check their values at the door when they show up for work. Over the next two days, I know you will reap the mutual benefit of your collective ideas and experiences.

## Three approaches to ethical dilemmas

As part of this conference, I understand you'll be examining the ethics programs of a number of companies. As you go through this exercise, you might find it useful to bear in mind the three very different approaches to dealing with ethical dilemmas that characterize how companies approach these ethics.

These are:

1) Neglect—or the absence of any formal ethical programs;

2) Compliance-based programs; and,

3) Values-oriented programs.

I'd like to spend a few moments touching on each of these three concepts.

It's hard to imagine that any large company could rationally ignore the importance of ethics or fail to develop management policies and programs given the effect ethical breaches can have on financial performance, sales and corporate reputation. But some companies clearly don't get the message.

According to the Institute for Crisis Management, more than one-half of the news crisis stories filed in 1993 were crises brought on by the questionable judgment of management—firings, white-collar crime, government investigations and discrimination suits. Coverage of these types of corporate misdeeds has risen 55 percent since 1989, while coverage of "operational" crises—chemical spills, product tamperings—has declined 4 percent.

Obviously, there are grave consequences for ignoring ethical problems. There is also increasing evidence from academic studies that show positive correlations between responsible business behavior and return-on-investment, stock price, consumer preferences and employee loyalty.

The companies that ignore ethics do so based on assumptions that are false and never challenged. They seem to view ethics either as unimportant or as a costly and inconvenient luxury.

I think they're wrong on both accounts.

I believe—and our company's experience demonstrates—that a company cannot sustain success unless it develops ways to anticipate and address ethical issues as they arise. Doing the right thing from Day One helps avoid future setbacks and regrets. Addressing ethical dilemmas when they arise may save your business from serious financial or reputational harm.

---

*Decisions which emphasize cost to the exclusion of all other factors don't serve a company's and its shareholders' long-term interests.*

---

Many companies share this view, and a number of them have chosen a second approach to ethics—what Lynn Sharp Paine, an associate professor at Harvard, refers to as compliance-based programs. These ethics programs are most often designed by corporate counsel. They are based on rules and regulations, with the goal of preventing, detecting and punishing legal violations.

Until recently, we were among the companies that took this approach. The centerpiece of our efforts was a comprehensive collection of regulations that spelled out our worldwide code of business ethics. In it, we laid out rules for hiring practices, travel and entertainment expenses, political contributions, compliance with local laws, improper payments, gifts and favors. We addressed topics ranging from accounting practices to potential conflicts of interest. As you might guess, it was a long and weighty list of do's and don't's for our people to follow.

This approach didn't serve us well. First, rules beget rules. And regulations beget regulations. We became buried in paperwork, and any time we faced a unique ethical issue, another rule or regulation was born. Second, our compliance-based program sent a disturbing message to our people—WE DON'T RESPECT YOUR INTELLIGENCE OR TRUST YOU! Finally, and one of the most compelling reasons for shedding this approach, it didn't keep managers or employees from exercising poor judgment and making questionable decisions.

We learned that you can't force ethical conduct into an organization. Ethics is a function of the collective attitudes of our people. And these attitudes are cultivated and supported by at least seven factors:

1) Commitment to responsible business conduct;
2) Management's leadership;
3) Trust in employees;
4) Programs and policies that provide people with clarity about the organization's ethical expectations;
5) Open, honest and timely communications;
6) Tools to help employees resolve ethical problems; and
7) Reward and recognition systems that reinforce the importance of ethics.

Ultimately, high ethical standards can be maintained only if they are modeled by management and woven into the fabric of the company. Knowing this, your challenge and mine is to cultivate the kind of environment where people do the right thing.

## Integrating values and individual responsibility

Realizing the importance of each of these elements led Levi Strauss & Co.—and a growing number of other companies—to try a third approach to ethics, based on a values orientation. This method combines functional values with individual responsibility and accountability.

Today, at Levi Strauss & Co., we base our approach to ethics upon six ethical principles—honesty, promise-keeping, fairness, respect for others, compassion and integrity.

Using this approach, we address ethical issues by first identifying which of these ethical principles applies to the particular business decision. Then, we determine which internal and which external stakeholders' ethical concerns should influence our business decisions. Information on stakeholder issues is gathered and possible recommendations are discussed with "high influence" stakeholder groups, such as shareholders, employees, customers, members of local communities, public interest groups, our business partners and so forth.

This principle-based approach balances the ethical concerns of these various stakeholders with the values of our organization. It is a process that extends trust to an individual's knowledge of the situation. It examines the complexity of issues that must be considered in each decision, and it defines the role each person's judgement plays in carrying out his or her responsibilities in an ethical manner.

We're integrating ethics with our other corporate values, which include diversity, open communications, empowerment, recognition, teamwork and honesty, into every aspect of our business—from our human resource practices to our relationships with our business partners.

I'd like to illustrate how we're linking ethics and business conduct with an area of increasing importance to many global corporations—the contract manufacturing of products in developing countries.

## Ethical guidelines for overseas sources

Because Levi Strauss & Co. operates in many countries and diverse cultures, we take special care in selecting contractors and those countries where our goods are produced. We do this to ensure that our products are being made in a manner consistent with our values and that protects our brand image and corporate reputation. So, in 1991, we developed a set of Global Sourcing Guidelines.

Our guidelines describe the business conduct we require of our contractors. For instance, the guidelines ban the use of child or prison labor. They stipulate certain environmental requirements. They limit working hours and mandate regularly scheduled days off. Workers must have the right of free association and not be exploited. At a minimum, wages must comply with the law and match prevailing local practice and working conditions must be safe and healthy. We also expect our business partners to be law abiding and to conduct all of their business affairs in an ethical way.

In developing our guidelines, we also recognized that there are certain issues beyond the control of our contractors, so we produced a list of "country selection" criteria. For example, we will not source in countries where conditions, such as the human rights climate, would run counter to our values and have an adverse effect on our global brand image or damage our corporate reputation.

Similarly, we will not source in countries where circumstances threaten our employees while traveling, where the legal climate makes it difficult or jeopardizes our trademarks, and where political or social turmoil threatens our commercial interest.

Since adopting our guidelines, we've terminated our business relationships with about 5 percent of our contractors and required workplace improvements of another 25 percent. Likewise, we announced a phased withdrawal from contracting in China and exited Burma due to human rights concerns, although we remain hopeful that the human rights climate in these countries will improve so we can alter these decisions.

---

*Ethics must trump all other considerations.*

---

In the process of creating our guidelines, we formed a working group of 15 employees from a broad cross section of the company. The working group spent nine months formulating our guidelines. In crafting these guidelines, they used our principle-based decision-making model to guide their deliberations.

Drafting these guidelines was difficult. Applying them has proven even more challenging.

When we were rolling out our guidelines—which included extensive on-site audits of each of our 700 contractors worldwide—we discovered that two of our manufacturing contractors in Bangladesh and one in Turkey employed underage workers. This was a clear violation of our guidelines, which prohibit the use of child labor. At the outset, it appeared that we had two options:

• Instruct our contractors to fire these children, knowing that many are the sole wage earners for their families and that if they lost their jobs, their families would face extreme hardships;

or we could:

• Continue to employ underage children, ignoring our stance against the use of child labor.

By referencing our ethical guidelines to decision making we came up with a different approach and one that we believe helped to minimize adverse ethical consequences.

The contractors agreed to pay the underage children their salaries and benefits while they go to school full-time. We agreed to pay for books, tuition and uniforms. When the children reach legal working age, they will be offered jobs in the plant. Due to these efforts, 35 children have attended school in Bangladesh, while another six are currently in school in Turkey.

And how did we benefit from this situation?

We were able to retain quality contractors that play an important role in our worldwide sourcing strategy. At the same time, we were able to honor our values and protect our brands.

Applying our sourcing guidelines has forced us to find creative solutions to vexing ethical dilemmas. Clearly, at times, adhering to these standards has added costs. To continue working for us, some contractors have added emergency exits and staircases, increased ventilation, reduced crowding, improved bathroom facilities and invested in water-treatment systems. The costs of these requirements have been passed on to us—at least in part—in the form of higher product prices. In other cases, we have foregone less expensive sources of production due to unsatisfactory working conditions or concerns about the country of origin.

Conventional wisdom holds that these added costs put us at a competitive disadvantage. Yes, they limit our options somewhat and squeeze profit margins in the near-term. But over the years, we've found that decisions which emphasize cost to the exclusion of all other factors don't serve a company's and its shareholders' long-term interests.

Moreover, as a company that invests hundreds of millions of advertising dollars each year to create consumer preference for our products, we have a huge stake in protecting that investment. In today's world, a television exposé on working conditions can undo years of effort to build brand loyalty. Why squander your investment when, with foresight and commitment, reputational problems can be prevented?

But you don't have to take my word for it.

There is a growing body of evidence that shows a positive correlation between good corporate citizenship and financial performance. Studies by leading research groups such as Opinion Research Corporation and Yankelovich Partners, respected scholars and socially responsible investment firms underscore the point that companies which look beyond solely maximizing wealth and profits and are driven by values and a sense of purpose outperform those companies that focus only on short-term gain.

Companies with strong corporate reputations have been shown to outperform the S&P 500, have higher sales, sustain greater profits and have stocks that outperform the market. These are results that no bottom-line fixated manager can ignore.

Similarly, a recent study suggests that how a company conducts itself affects consumer purchasing decisions and customer loyalty. A vast majority—84 percent—of the American public agrees that a company's reputation can well be the deciding factor in terms of what product or service they buy.

These findings mirror our own experience. Our values-driven approach has helped us:

• Identify contractors who want to work for Levi Strauss & Co. to achieve our "blue ribbon" certification, enhancing their own business stature;

• We have gained retailer and consumer loyalty. Retailers feel good about having us as business partners because of our commitment to ethical practices. Today's consumer has more products to choose from and more information about those products. A company's reputation forms a part of the consumer's perceptions of the product and influences purchasing decisions.

At the same time:

• We're better able to attract, retain and motivate the most-talented employees, because the company's values more closely mirror their own personal values.

• Because government and community leaders view us as a responsible corporate citizen we have been welcomed to do business in established and emerging markets.

Let me conclude with a few last thoughts.

We are living in an environment in which ethical standards and behaviors are being increasingly challenged. Addressing these dilemmas becomes even more difficult when you overlay the complexities of different cultures and values systems that exist throughout the world. For example, in some cultures honesty will take precedence over caring—"tell the truth even if it hurts"; whereas other cultures find caring, or "saving face" as the predominant value.

As you grapple with some fictitious ethical quandaries over the next two days, I encourage you to ask yourselves these questions:

• "How much am I willing to compromise my principles?"

• "Are there times when I'm willing to risk something I value for doing the right thing?"

For me and my associates at Levi Strauss & Co. I think the answers have become clear: Ethics must trump all other considerations. Ultimately, there are important commercial benefits to be gained from managing your business in a responsible and ethical way that best serves your enterprise's long-term interests. The opposite seems equally clear: the dangers of not doing so are profound.

Michael Josephson, a noted ethics expert, defined ethics this way: "Ethics is about character and courage and how we meet the challenge when doing the right thing will cost more than we want to pay."

The good news is that courage carries with it a great reward—the prospect of sustained responsible commercial success. I think that's what each of us wants our legacy to be. And I believe ultimately our key stakeholders—all of them—will accept nothing less.

# 11

# Ceos Are Paid What They Are Worth

Darryl C. Salas

*Darryl C. Salas, a former manager at Ford Motor Company, is an attorney with Leydig, Voit & Mayer, Ltd., in Chicago.*

Although the American public is critical of the pay levels of chief executive officers at a time when many people are being laid off, there is no reliable evidence that CEOs are overpaid. Studies comparing American and Japanese CEO pay are inconclusive since the executives operate in different markets. The comparisons are also faulty because while Japanese CEOS are paid less than their American counterparts, the Japanese executives often receive lifetime job security and pay, factors not found in U.S. corporations. Government attempts to cap executive pay are irresponsible and could lead to America's best managers' leaving for other markets that pay more.

When Ben & Jerry's Ben Cohen stepped down in July 1994 as the company's chief executive, he announced that his replacement would be paid far more than he had been. With the hiring of the new CEO, Ben & Jerry's, known for its socially responsible business programs, will abandon the pay scale it had instituted to ensure that no employee would be paid more than seven times that of the lowest-paid worker's salary, currently $23,000. Cohen and his partner recognized that compensation for running a company the size of Ben & Jerry's (projected $1 billion in sales by the year 2000) would have to be much higher in order to attract a qualified CEO.

Ben and Jerry are not alone in feeling the pressure of rising standards of executive compensation. *Business Week* has reported that from 1984 to 1994 CEO pay grew four times faster than the pay of the average worker and three times faster than corporate profits. Even as the real pay (accounting for inflation) of the average American worker has slipped by almost 13 percent between 1970 and 1990, the pay of CEOs has increased almost four times. Contrasting the picture painted by the preceding fig-

Darryl C. Salas, "Are Top Executives Paid Too Much?" *Business and Society Review*, Summer 1994. Reprinted with permission.

## The top 20 highest-paid chief executives in 1993

| Name and company | Salary and bonus | Long-term compensation | Total pay |
|---|---|---|---|
| 1. Michael D. Eisner Walt Disney | $750,000 | $202,261,000 | $203,011,000 |
| 2. Sanford I. Weill Travelers | 4,291,000 | 48,519,000 | 52,810,000 |
| 3. Joseph R. Hyde III Autozone | 1,103,000 | 31,117,000 | 32,220,000 |
| 4. Charles N. Mathewson Int. Game Tech. | 628,000 | 21,603,000 | 22,231,000 |
| 5. Alan C. Greenberg Bear Stearns | 11,988,000 | 3,927,000 | 15,915,000 |
| 6. H. Wayne Huizenga Blockbuster Ent. | 557,000 | 15,000,000 | 15,557,000 |
| 7. Norman E. Brinker Brinker Intl. | 1,338,000 | 13,587,000 | 14,925,000 |
| 8. Roberto C. Goizueta Coca-Cola | 3,654,000 | 10,859,000 | 14,513,000 |
| 9. C. Robert Kidder Duracell Intl. | 1,038,000 | 13,134,000 | 14,172,000 |
| 10. Thomas M. Hahn Jr. Georgia-Pacific | 12,243,000 | 1,437,000 | 13,680,000 |
| 11. H. Brewster Atwater Jr. General Mills | 1,386,000 | 11,791,000 | 13,177,000 |
| 12. James C. Morgan Applied Materials | 1,509,000 | 11,324,000 | 12,833,000 |
| 13. Richard H. Jenrette Equitable Cos. | 12,130,000 | 250,000 | 12,380,000 |
| 14. Harry A. Merlo Louisiana-Pacific | 745,000 | 11,306,000 | 12,051,000 |
| 15. John H. Bryan Sara Lee | 1,886,000 | 10,003,000 | 11,889,000 |
| 16. David R. Whitwam Whirlpool | 2,100,000 | 9,737,000 | 11,837,000 |
| 17. Charles S. Sanford Jr. Bankers Trust | 8,865,000 | 2,945,000 | 11,811,000 |
| 18. Frank V. Cahouet Mellon Bank | 1,391,000 | 10,125,000 | 11,516,000 |
| 19. Walter J. Sanders III Adv. Micro Devices | 3,212,000 | 8,276,000 | 11,488,000 |
| 20. Stanley C. Gault Goodyear | 1,986,000 | 9,292,000 | 11,278,000 |

Source: *Business Week*, April 25, 1994.

ures, a report in the *Harvard Business Review* in 1990 concluded that, when adjusted for inflation, CEO pay levels by 1988 were just catching up to where they were 50 years ago.

Whatever position one takes, it cannot be denied that in a time of layoffs and a weak economy, public discontent with exorbitant CEO salaries has been rising. The heightened negative publicity that the issue of executive compensation has been receiving makes it an easy target for politicians. The Securities and Exchange Commission (SEC) has responded to the controversy by increasing disclosure requirements regarding executive compensation. These requirements make an executive's total compensation value more clear to shareholders. Following the SEC's passage of the new detailed disclosure requirements, Congress passed legislation which requires companies to design performance-related, nondiscretionary compensation packages in order to receive corporate deductions for executive compensation exceeding $1 million.

## Structural flaws of organizations

To some degree, the perception of a noncompetitive executive labor market can be attributed to several structural problems inherent to business organization. Many scholars argue that the board members who decide the CEO's compensation are biased in the CEO's favor. Board members are likely to be either company insiders whom the CEO can fire, or outsiders whom the CEO has picked as representatives of shareholder interests. These outsiders, in turn, are likely to be CEOs of other large public companies, or "professional" directors who sit on many boards. These board members and the CEO may cooperate to protect each other's interests.

Another possible organizational flaw leading to executive overcompensation is the absence of accurate standards of performance for CEOs. Once a CEO is running a company, most of the information a board receives on his performance comes from the CEO himself. Boards of directors hire a new chief or retain an old one based on very little information. The CEO may also hire outside compensation consultants, who find themselves in the compromising position of being paid by the people whose salaries they are supposed to evaluate. In addition, because board members seldom own significant amounts of stock, their personal finances do not wax and wane with corporate performance. "There's no external mechanism, short of bankruptcy, that penalizes a board for foolish compensation decisions or for lax oversight," said Joseph A. Grundfest in an April 1992 *Scientific American* interview.

What appears to undermine the foregoing arguments is the theory that the stock market keeps the executive labor market disciplined. That is, if shareholders become dissatisfied with management, they can sell their shares. The resulting drop in the price of the firm's stock will also harm the firm's managers, who typically have a substantial portion of their personal wealth linked to the firm through stock options, stock ownership, and incentive compensation plans.

## No convincing evidence they are overpaid

Because there are no reliable surveys that compare how much executives are paid versus the minimum that they would be willing to receive to do the same job, alternative measures must be devised. In 1993, Professor Lambert of Stanford University and Professors Larcker and Weigelt of the University of Pennsylvania tested various hypotheses representing structural models of managerial compensation. They found that an executive's compensation will be an increasing function of managerial power. In other words, the CEO may be able to negotiate a high salary because: (1) he can influence the board of directors; (2) the shareholders trust him and

are willing to pay a premium for his services; or (3) the pay structure creates a sort of managerial tournament that leads to increased competition
and performance among managers within a company.

Another possible measure of executive pay is comparison of American and Japanese salaries. This measure produces inconclusive evidence
and lends weak support, if any, to the thesis that U.S. executives are overpaid, since the executives operate in different markets. A May 1992 study
in *Time* magazine found that while the average Japanese CEO earns
$400,000 in annual pay and the typical head of a German corporation
earns about $800,000 a year, most heads of major U.S. companies make
$1 million to $4 million a year. However, Japanese executives receive

## Fantasyland Payday for Disney CEO

Linking pay to performance does not necessarily keep the lid on skyrocketing
CEO compensation. Legislation passed in 1993 to tax corporate salaries exceeding
$1 million per year was designed to encourage performance-based pay strategies.
But for Michael D. Eisner, chairman of The Walt Disney Company and 1993's
highest-paid CEO, the new legislation inspired some strategic financing, but did
nothing to prevent him from earning a record $203 million income last year.

Eisner received a minimal salary (*only* $750,000 in 1993) but earned millions
from stock options and other incentives received as part of his total compensation package. Disney can deduct whatever it pays Eisner because, with the excep-
tion of his relatively small salary, all of his pay is based on performance. That is
true of his stock options as well as an incentive plan that entitles him to a bonus
equal to 2 percent of Disney's after-tax profits in excess of 11 percent return on
equity, *Business Week* reported.

On November 30, 1993, Eisner realized a record $197 million stock option
gain. Eisner exercised options on 5.4 million shares of Disney stock granted as far
back as 1984. He realized $202,260,592 from that transaction at the beginning of
Disney's 1993 fiscal year. Eisner's remaining stock options are worth $161.4 million.

Has Disney's performance merited such astronomical rewards for its CEO? In
the short term, Disney's performance has been disappointing. The company's net
income fell last year by 63 percent, to $299.8 million, due in part to the Euro-
Disney disaster. But in the long term, the picture brightens considerably. Since
Eisner joined Disney as CEO in 1984, Disney's total market value has risen from
$2.2 billion to $22.7 billion in 1994. A shareholder who bought $100 of Disney
stock in 1984 would now have $1,640.

Yet some observers are not convinced that the new $1 million limit on de-
ductibility is effective. Only 2 percent of the variation in CEO packages in 1992
could be explained by the difference in company performance at the 180 largest
corporations, *Business Week* reported. And the gap between executive and laborer
salaries is still enormous. Last year the average CEO of a major company made
149 times that of the average factory worker's pay—a difference in average salaries
of $25,317 versus $3,841,273.

Disney, along with many other companies, argues that it is unfair to include
gains that result from the exercise of stock options granted a decade ago in a single year's pay. *Business Week* notes, however, that the repeated appearance of Eisner on its top 20 list argues that such gains are virtually annual events. Raymond
L. Watson, head of Disney's compensation committee, believes the company's
original deal with Eisner was flawed because all of his stock options were priced
at market value when at least some could have been priced at a premium. "None
of us in our wildest dreams ever imagined we'd be looking at a $200 million pay-
day. But then again, we never thought we'd be talking about a market cap of $22
billion either."

many benefits not found in U.S. corporations, such as lifetime job security and lifetime pay. In addition, Japanese companies typically use a
team-management approach that makes the CEO a much less vital component of management.

Although it may be politically tempting to attack executive salaries at
a time when the average American has to worry about layoffs, any arbi-
trary tinkering with the system would be irresponsible. (The idea of setting pay caps on CEO salaries was proposed by Rep. Martin O. Sabo of
Minnesota in 1991.) Rather than require a manager's performance to be
aligned with his pay, this plan would arbitrarily put a cap on executive
pay so that good managers would be paid the same amount as bad managers. Because management salaries are only a small part of firms' cost
structure, there is correspondingly only a small potential for this type of
action to have a positive effect. It is possible that a pay cap would have
no effect at all except to change the form of management. For example,
American businesses could respond by adopting the Japanese style of
management and have shared responsibility at the top. Instead of having
one CEO making $1 million, firms would have three CEOs each making
$333,000. Finally, pay caps could have profoundly negative effects on
firms. One such potential effect could be that corporate America could
lose its best talent to other labor markets that pay more. In a 1990 *Harvard Business Review* article, Michael C. Jensen and Kevin J. Murphy argue
that compensation of executives is modest in comparison with compensation of top-level partners in law firms or the most successful Wall Street
players. The authors contend that "the relentless focus on how much
CEOs are paid diverts public attention from the real problem—how CEOs
are paid." Considering how much money a corporation can lose as a result of one bad decision, it is not hard to imagine the profound effect that
this talent flight would have on the economy.

> *When adjusted for inflation, CEO pay levels by
> 1988 were just catching up to where they were 50
> years ago.*

The SEC responded to public pressure in 1992 by adopting amendments to the executive compensation disclosure requirements. The
changes require companies to provide stockholders with clearer details
about how executives are paid and how that pay relates to the company's
stock performance. In addition, companies must disclose information regarding potential organizational structure flaws such as insiders involved
with compensation committees and interlocking directorships. Since
there is no convincing evidence that the executive-labor market is ineffi-
cient, the general effect of the new amendments may be limited with respect to how much executives are paid. However, if some executives are
overpaid, these disclosure requirements could have a dramatic effect, especially if shareholders such as pension funds and institutional investors
control a significant amount of shares in the company. In addition, the
detailed information revealed will facilitate more reliable empirical studies in the future. The main criticism of these disclosure requirements is

that they add to the cost of doing business by making disclosure even more complicated than it already is, and by increasing the potential for inadvertent securities laws violations for misstatements or omissions of "material" facts.

Following the lead of the SEC, Congress passed an initiative in 1993 to disallow corporate deductions for executive compensation that exceeds $1 million unless the money is paid according to a nondiscretionary performance plan that is ratified by the shareholders. In situations where executives are being overpaid, this law is likely to be even more effective than the SEC's measures because it involves shareholders in the vote on executive compensation. In addition, it is likely to put pressure on corporations to reduce discretionary compensation. Though a corporation can forgo the deduction, a public corporation may find it embarrassing to report that the compensation of its top executives is not fully deductible.

Whether or not top executives are overpaid, it seems that the executive labor market is balanced by the opposing forces of structural flaws in organizations (such as biased board members), the effects of large stockholders (who may react unfavorably to excessive CEO salaries), and incentive plans that tie executive pay to the performance of the company. Although few economists agree on the best approach, there seems to be a general consensus that large firms perform better when a mixture of long-term and short-term incentive plans are adopted, rather than no incentives at all. The combination of the two ensures that executives will not manipulate company policies for their own profit. In short, the problem seems to be how executives are paid, not how much.

# Organizations to Contact

The editors have compiled the following list of organizations concerned with the issues debated in this book. The descriptions are derived from materials provided by the organizations. All have publications or information available for interested readers. The list was compiled on the date of publication of the present volume; names, addresses, and phone numbers may change. Be aware that many organizations take several weeks or longer to respond to inquiries, so allow as much time as possible.

**American Economic Foundation (AEF)**
50 Public Square, Suite 1300
Cleveland, OH 44113
(216) 321-6547

The foundation is a nonprofit research and educational organization that advocates free-market economic principles. It publishes the economic primer *How We Live*, the leaflet *Ten Pillars of Economic Wisdom*, and various booklets and pamphlets related to the private enterprise system.

**Brookings Institution**
1775 Massachusetts Ave. NW
Washington, DC 20036-2188
(202) 797-6000

The institution is a private, nonprofit organization devoted to research, education, and publication in economics, business, government, foreign policy, and the social sciences. Its principal purpose is to contribute informed perspectives on the current and emerging public policy issues facing the American people. Its publications include the *Brookings Review*.

**Canadian Coalition for Ecology, Ethics and Religion (CCEER)**
22 Carriage Bay
Winnipeg, MB R2Y 0M5
CANADA
(204) 832-1882
fax: (204) 885-6105

CCEER is a national organization that focuses on spiritual and ethical concerns regarding the environment and conservation. It developed a Canadian and a global network of environmental, academic, and religious organizations and individuals to support environmental ethics, issues, and education. The coalition provides a clearinghouse for information and publishes the bimonthly newsletter *Sacred Spaces*.

**Cato Institute**
224 Second St. SE
Washington, DC 20003
(202) 546-0200

The institute is a libertarian public policy research organization that works to limit government intervention in the economy. The institute publishes the *Cato Journal* and various books and reports.

94

**Center for Applied Christian Ethics (CACE)**
Wheaton College
Wheaton, IL 60187
(708) 752-5886

The goal of CACE is to raise moral awareness and elicit moral thinking by encouraging the application of Christian ethics to public policy and personal practice. The center's activities and publications focus on ethics in business management, public policy, biomedical research, communications, and the arts. Its publications include the newsletter *Discernment* and the booklets *Understanding and Responding to Moral Pluralism* and *Sin of Greed and the Spirit of Christian Generosity*.

**Center for Ethics Studies**
Marquette University
Academic Support Facility 336
Milwaukee, WI 53233
(414) 288-5824

Marquette University is a Jesuit educational institution. The primary goal of the Center for Ethics Studies is to be an ethics resource for the university and the community at large. A clearinghouse for ethics information, the center publishes *Ethics of Free Enterprise: Values in Jesuit Education, Ethics Across the Curriculum,* and *Teaching Ethics: An Interdisciplinary Approach*.

**Common Cause**
2030 M St. NW
Washington, DC 20036
(202) 833-1200
fax: (202) 659-3716

Common Cause is a liberal lobbying organization that works to improve the ethical standards of Congress and government in general. Its priorities include campaign reform, making government officials accountable for their actions, and promoting civil rights for all citizens. Common Cause publishes the quarterly *Common Cause Magazine* in addition to position papers and reports.

**The Conference Board**
845 Third Ave.
New York, NY 10022
(212) 759-0900

This fact-finding institution conducts research and publishes studies on business economics and management. Its Work and Family Information Center researches changes in work and family relationships. Its publications include the monthly journal *Across the Board* and *Conference Board Briefing*.

**Council on Economic Priorities (CEP)**
30 Irving Pl.
New York, NY 10003
(212) 420-1133
(800) 822-4237

CEP is a nonprofit public interest research organization that evaluates and reports on the policies and practices of U.S. and foreign corporations in the areas of the environment, women and minority advancement, disclosure, charitable giving and community outreach, family benefits, and workplace issues. It publishes the books *Shopping for a Better World* and *Students Shopping for a Better World*, the monthly newsletter *Research Report*, and corporate environmental data reports.

### Ethics Resource Center
1120 G St. NW, Suite 200
Washington, DC 20005
(202) 434-8468

The center is a nonprofit organization working to foster integrity, ethical conduct, and basic values in the nation's institutions. It sponsors programs and develops materials on ethics and character education for children and adults and advises business, government, professional, and trade organizations on how to promote high standards of ethical conduct. The center publishes the quarterly *Ethics Journal* and the survey report *Ethics Policies and Programs in American Business*. It also produces the video *Not for Sale* and the video series *Ethics at Work*.

### Foundation for Economic Education (FEE)
Irvington-on-Hudson, NY 10533
(914) 591-7230

FEE supports private property, the free market, and limited government. It frequently publishes articles on trade, capitalism, and corporate social responsibility in its monthly magazine the *Freeman*.

### The Heritage Foundation
214 Massachusetts Ave. NE
Washington, DC 20002
(202) 546-4400

The Heritage Foundation is a conservative public policy organization that supports free enterprise, supply-side economics, and limited government. Its publications include the monthly *Policy Review*, the Backgrounder series of occasional papers, and the Heritage Lecture series.

### Institute for Global Ethics
PO Box 563
Camden, ME 04843
(207) 236-6658

The institute is a nonprofit research and educational organization. Its goal is to discover and articulate ethical values, to analyze ethical trends, and to gather and disseminate information on global ethics. It sponsors programs, seminars, workshops, and lectures and publishes the monthly *Insights on Global Ethics*, the periodic newsletter *News Flash*, the book *Global Ethics: Common Values for a Shrinking World*, and the videotape *Personal Ethics and the Future of the World*.

**Josephson Institute of Ethics**
4640 Admiralty Way, Suite 1001
Marina del Rey, CA 90292
(213) 306-1868
fax: (213) 827-1864

The institute is a nonprofit membership organization founded to improve the ethical quality of society by teaching and advocating principled reasoning and ethical decision making. Its Government Ethics Center has conducted programs and workshops for more than twenty thousand influential leaders. The institute's publications include the periodic newsletter *Ethics in Action*, the quarterly *Ethics: Easier Said Than Done*, and reports such as *Ethics of American Youth: A Warning and a Call to Action*.

**The Park Ridge Center for the Study of Health, Faith, and Ethics**
211 E. Ontario St., Suite 800
Chicago, IL 60611-3215
(312) 266-2222
fax: (312) 266-6086

The center explores the relationships between health, faith, and ethics, focusing on the religious dimensions of illness and health. It seeks to help clergy, health care professionals, ethicists, educators, and public policymakers to address ethical issues and create ethical policies. The center publishes the quarterly *Second Opinion*, the newsletter *Centerline*, and the book series Health and Medicine in the Faith Traditions.

# Bibliography

## Books

Connie Bruck           *The Predators' Ball: The Junk-Bond Raiders and the Man Who Staked Them.* New York: The American Lawyer/Simon & Schuster, 1988.

Gerald F. Cavanagh     *American Business Values.* 3rd ed. Englewood Cliffs, NJ: Prentice Hall, 1990.

Ralph W. Clark and     *Workplace Ethics.* Lanham, MD: University Press of
Alice Darnell Lattal   America, 1992.

Barry Commoner         *Making Peace with the Planet.* New York: Pantheon, 1990.

David E. Cooper and    *The Environment in Question: Ethics and Global Issues.*
Joy A. Palmer, eds.    New York: Routledge, 1992.

Joseph W. Cotchett     *The Ethics Gap—Greed and the Casino Society: The*
and Stephen P. Pizzo   *Erosion of Ethics in Our Professions, Business, and Government.* Carlsbad, CA: Parker & Son, 1991.

Graef S. Crystal       *In Search of Excess: The Overcompensation of American Executives.* New York: Norton, 1991.

Richard T. DeGeorge    *Business Ethics.* 3rd ed. New York: Macmillan, 1990.

David Dembo,           *Abuse of Power—Social Performance of Multinational*
Ward Morehouse,        *Corporations: The Case of Union Carbide.* New York: New
and Lucinda Wykle      Horizons Press, 1990.

Owen Edwards           *Upward Nobility: How to Succeed in Business Without Losing Your Soul.* New York: Crown, 1991.

O.C. Ferrell and       *In Pursuit of Ethics: Tough Choices in the World of Work.*
Gareth Gardiner        Springfield, IL: Smith Collins, 1991.

R. Edward Freeman,     *Business Ethics: The State of the Art.* New York: Oxford
ed.                    University Press, 1991.

Robert P. George       *Making Men Moral: Civil Liberties and Public Morality.* New York: Oxford University Press, Clarendon Press, 1994.

Brian Harvey, ed.      *Business Ethics: A European Approach.* New York: Prentice Hall, 1994.

William D. Hitt        *Ethics and Leadership: Putting Theory into Practice.* Columbus, OH: Battelle Press, 1990.

Jane Jacobs            *A System of Survival: A Dialogue on the Moral Foundations of Commerce and Politics.* New York: Random House, 1992.

John A. Jenkins        *The Litigators: Inside the Powerful World of America's High-Stakes Trial Lawyers.* New York: Doubleday, 1989.

Rushworth M. Kidder   *How Good People Make Tough Choices: Resolving the Dilemmas of Ethical Living.* New York: William Morrow, 1995.

James S. Kunen   *Reckless Disregard: Corporate Greed, Government Indifference, and the Kentucky School Bus Crash.* New York: Simon & Schuster, 1994.

Fred Lager   *Ben & Jerry's—the Inside Scoop: How Two Real Guys Built a Business with a Social Conscience and a Sense of Humor.* New York: Crown, 1994.

James E. Liebig   *Business Ethics: Profiles in Civic Virtue.* Golden, CO: Fulcrum Publishing, 1990.

Peter Madsen and   *Essentials of Business Ethics.* New York: Penguin, 1990.
Jay M. Shafritz, eds.

Walter W. Manley II   *Critical Issues in Business Conduct: Legal, Ethical, and Social*
and William A. Shrode   *Challenges for the 1990s.* Westport, CT: Quorum Books, 1990.

Mary Midgley   *Can't We Make Moral Judgements?* New York: St. Martin's Press, 1991.

Morton Mintz   *At Any Cost: Corporate Greed, Women, and the Dalkon Shield.* New York: Pantheon, 1985.

Kai Nielsen   *Ethics Without God.* Rev. ed. Buffalo: Prometheus, 1990.

Randy Pennington   *On My Honor I Will: How One Simple Oath Can Lead You*
and Marc Bockmon   *to Success in Business.* New York: Warner Books, 1992.

Alan Reder   *The Pursuit of Principle and Profit: Business Success Through Social Responsibility.* New York: Putnam, 1994.

Jeffrey K. Salkin   *Being God's Partner: How to Find the Hidden Link Between Spirituality and Your Work.* Woodstock, VT: Jewish Lights Publishing, 1994.

Barry Siegel   *Shades of Gray: Ordinary People in Extraordinary Circumstances.* New York: Bantam, 1992.

Adam Smith   *An Inquiry into the Nature and Causes of the Wealth of Nations.* New York: Oxford University Press, 1993.

Robert Solomon   *Ethics and Excellence: Cooperation and Integrity in Business.* New York: Oxford University Press, 1992.

Charles E. Watson   *Managing with Integrity: Insights from America's CEOs.* New York: Praeger, 1991.

## Periodicals

Dexter F. Baker   "Ethical Issues and Decision Making in Business," *Vital Speeches of the Day*, January 15, 1993.

David Barsamian   "Corporate Power: Profits Before People," *Z Magazine*, February 1995.

Brent Bozell   "Corporations Work to Advance Leftist Causes," *Conservative Chronicle*, August 11, 1993. Available from PO Box 29, Hampton, IA 50441.

John A. Byrne

"Executive Pay: Compensation at the Top Is Out of Control. Here's How to Reform It," *Business Week*, March 30, 1992.

Edward T. Chase

"Smoking, Health, and Hypocrisy," *Nation*, March 20, 1995.

Richard Cohen

"Trashing Employees for Higher Dividends," *Liberal Opinion Week*, September 6, 1993. Available from PO Box 468, Vinton, IA 52349.

Michael Elliott

"Corruption: How Bribes, Payoffs, and Crooked Officials Are Blocking Economic Growth," *Newsweek*, November 14, 1994.

*Ethics: Easier Said Than Done*

Entire issue on business ethics, no. 22, 1993. Available from 4640 Admiralty Way, Suite 1001, Marina del Rey, CA 90292-6610.

Amitai Etzioni

"Corporate Behavior: Fewer Flaws Mean Fewer Laws," *Business and Society Review*, Spring 1992. Available from 25-13 Old Kings Highway N., Suite 107, Darien, CT 06820.

*Financial World*

Entire issue on business ethics, Fall 1994. Available from 1328 Broadway, New York, NY 10001.

David D. Haddock

"Is Insider Trading Really Wrong?" *Fortune*, October 18, 1993.

John Hasnas

"The Social Responsibility of Corporations and How to Make It Work for You," *Freeman*, July 1994. Available from the Foundation for Economic Education, Irvington-on-Hudson, New York 10533.

Laurence H. Kallen

"Bankruptcy Bailouts: Megacorporations and Chapter 11," *Multinational Monitor*, January/February 1993.

Skip Kaltenheuser

"China: Doing Business Under an Immoral Government," *Business Ethics*, May/June 1995. Available from 52 S. 10th St., #110, Minneapolis, MN 55403-2001.

Coretta Scott King

"Social Responsibility Is Good Business," *Liberal Opinion Week*, February 7, 1994.

Jonathan Kozol

"Kids as Commodities: The Folly of For-Profit Schools," *Business and Society Review*, Winter 1993.

Dwight R. Lee and Richard B. McKenzie

"How the Marketplace Fosters Business Honesty," *Business and Society Review*, Winter 1995.

David Moberg

"Suite Crimes," *In These Times*, December 12, 1993.

William Murchison

"Selling Rope to the Hangman," *Conservative Chronicle*, January 12, 1994.

Ralph Nader

"Corporate Welfare," *Liberal Opinion Week*, January 17, 1994.

Marvin Olaskey

"Corporate Giving Empowers People," *Insight*, June 13, 1994. Available from 3600 New York Ave. NE, Washington, DC 20002.

| | |
|---|---|
| Robert Payton | "Philanthropy Isn't Solely Good Will," *Insight*, June 13, 1994. |
| David E. Provost | "Corporate Responsibility," *Christian Century*, April 7, 1993. |
| Anita Roddick | "For the Common Good," *Resurgence*, September/ October 1994. Available from 33 E. Minor St., Emmaus, PA 18049. |
| Robert J. Samuelson | "R.I.P.: The Good Corporation," *Newsweek*, July 5, 1993. |
| Mary Scott and Howard Rothman | "Companies with a Conscience," *World Monitor*, October 1992. Available from Christian Science Publishing Society, One Norway St., Boston, MA 02115. |
| David Segal | "The Filtered Truth," *Washington Monthly*, September 1993. |
| Menlo Smith | "Should Corporations Be Charitable?" *Business and Society Review*, Spring 1994. |
| *Utne Reader* | "The Business of Business? The Meaning, Limits, and Promise of Socially Responsible Business," September/October 1993. |
| Harry J. Van Buren III | "Business Ethics for the New Millennium," *Business and Society Review*, Spring 1995. |
| *World & I* | "Journalism on the Rocks?" entire section on media ethics, December 1993. Available from 3600 New York Ave. NE, Washington, DC 20002. |

# Index

accounting
  considers only bottom line, 30
    should include more, 31-33
    stakeholder, 31-32
American Honda, 80
American Law Institute (ALI), 39-40, 43
*American Lawyer*, 66
Araskog, Rand, 58
Aristotle, 36, 53, 67
*Aronson v. Lewis*, 42
asbestos, 45-46
athletes, professional. *See* sports stars
Atwater, H. Brewster, 89
auditor, original meaning of, 31
Audubon Associates, 24
Aveda, 25
Avon Products, 57

Bandow, Doug, 72
Ben & Jerry's, 23, 88
Berle, A., 39
The Body Shop, 23, 25
Border Industrialization Program
  (Mexico), 46-48
bovine growth hormone (BGH), 25
Brinker, Norman E., 89
Bryan, John H., 89
Bush, George, 54-55
business
  socially responsible behaviors in, 20-21
  subgoals of, 18-19
  *see also* corporations
Business Committee for the Arts, 38
Business Enterprise Trust, 19
Businesses for Social Responsibility, 24
business ethics. *See* ethics
*Business Ethics* (Hoffman and Moore,
  eds.), 71
*Business Ethics* (McGee, ed.), 71
*Business Ethics* magazine, 28
*Business Week*, 88, 91
Butler, Samuel, 59

Cahouet, Frank V., 89
Canseco, Jose, 59, 60, 62-63
*Capitalism and Freedom* (Friedman), 17
Capital Research Center, 78
cause-related marketing, 78
CEOs
  are overpaid, 53-66
    comparison with Japan, 58-59
    examples of, 57-58

are paid what they are worth, 88-93
  due to organizational flaws, 90
  workers' pay raises compared, 88-89
history of pay increases, 56-57
international attempts at pay control,
  55
nondiscretionary performance plan, 93
pay, compared with
  entertainers, 56, 59, 64-65
  investment bankers, 56, 59, 65-66
  lawyers, 56, 59, 66
  sports stars, 56, 59, 60-63
and SEC disclosure requirements,
  92-93
cheap labor, as relocation reason, 44-45
chief executive officers. *See* CEOs
*Chronicle of Philanthropy*, 38, 42
Chrysler Corporation, 47
Cin-Made Corporation, 28
Clemens, Roger, 60
Code of Conduct on Transnational
  Corporations (U.N.), 51
Cohen, Ben, 88
Coizueta, Roberto C., 89
comparable worth, and CEO pay, 59-60
compliance-based programs
  and ethical dilemmas, 82, 83-84
Coors, Jeffrey H., 76
Corporate Accountability Commission,
  32
corporate executives
  are business owners' agents, 12-13
  legal cases on responsibilities of, 42
  *see also* CEOs
Corporate Governance Project, 40, 43
*Corporate Philanthropy Report*, 38, 42, 43
corporations
  are responsible only to owners, 12-13,
    72-75
  changed structure of, 38-40
  must serve public interest, 30-31
  and philanthropy, 34-43
  structural flaws in, 90
  *see also* CEOs; corporate social
    responsibility
corporate social responsibility
  benefits business, 18-29
  con, 67-71
  vs. "the bottom line," 30-33
  definition/meaning of, 19-21
  and duty vs. interest, 67-69
  Friedman's case against, 11-17

# 104    At Issue

Scientific American, 90
Secretariat of Urban Development and
  Ecology (SEDUE; Mexico), 50
Securities and Exchange Commission
  (SEC)
  as Corporate Accountability
    Commission, 32
  disclosure requirements, 92-93
Serle, A., 39
Shaw, Bill, 34
"shelter programs" of maquiladoras, 48
Sierra magazine, 26
Smith, Adam, 15, 68
Smith v. Van Gorkom (1985), 42
socialism, corporate social responsibility
  as, 11-12, 17
Social Venture Network (SVN), 19, 24
Socrates, 35
Sony, 47
sourcing, guidelines for overseas, 84-86
South Shore Bank, 25
Southwest Airlines, 26
Souza, Ed, 24
Spielberg, Steven, 64
Sporting News, 60
sports stars, comparative pay of, 56, 59,
  60-63
Springfield Remanufacturing, 28
stakeholder(s), 69, 87
  accounting, 31-32
Stonyfield Farm, 23-25, 28
Stride Rite Corporation, 21, 28
structural flaws in organizations, 90

Task Force on Private Sector Initiatives
  (1981), 73
taxes
  as pay control, 55
  without representation,
    corporate social responsibility is,
    13-14
TDK,47
Texas Water Commission, 48
Thatcher, Margaret, 55
theft, corporate social responsibility is,
  16, 72
Thoreau, Henry David, 81
Time Inc., 61

Time magazine, 91
Time Warner, 57
Tom's of Maine, 25

unions, wage restraint by, 15
United Nations
  Code of Conduct on Transnational
    Corporations, 51
  Environment Programme, 45, 51
  World Health Organization (WHO), 51
United Technologies, 47, 51
utilitarianism, 35-37
  and self-interest, 42

values-oriented programs
  also known as
    principles-based approach, 84, 85
    values-driven programs, 84, 86
  as approach to ethical dilemmas, 82,
    84
virtue ethics, 35
von Hayek, Friedrich A., 74

wage(s)
  control, 16-17
    failure of, 54
  minimum, 72
  restraint, by unions, 15
Waldron, Hicks, 57
Wall Street Journal, 65
Walt Disney Company, 58, 61, 91
Warner Communications, 61
Wasserstein, Bruce, 59, 65
Wasserstein Perella & Co., 65
Watson, Raymond L., 91
Weill, Sanford D., 89
Whitwam, David R., 89
working conditions, and multinationals,
  45-46, 49-50
working hours, control of, 72
World Bank, 51
World Health Organization (WHO), 51
W.R. Grace, 57

Yankelovich Partners, 86
Yazaki, 47

Zenith, 47